THE CRUDE OIL ADVENTURE
OF THE
HUMAN RE-EVOLUTION

The Crude Oil Adventure of the Human Re-Evolution
Copyright 2011 *by Kim A Schulz*
All Right Reserved

Published 2012
2nd Edition Published 2014
by WoMenHead101

ISBN #
978-0-578-09991-0

Dedicated to
All those who have helped me on my journey.
Living and dead.
Thank you for your love and your patience.
Especially my best friend and wife, Celia.

Also a Special Thank You to
Sharon Renae & Maia Rizzi for
sharing your wisdom

TABLE OF CONTENTS

Forward	Page 1
Introduction	Page 3
Chapter One – The Year 2010	Page 13
Chapter Two – 2011 The Rapture	Page 31
Chapter Three – 2011 The Beach	Page 51
Chapter Four - The Year 2012	Page 63
Chapter Five – The Year 2013	Page 75
Chapter Six – Conclusion (Faith)	Page 109
In Honor of	Page 115
Maps	Page 116
Online Reference Guide	Page 118

Forward

This book was originally written in the year 2011. The second edition was composed in the year 2014. In most part, it's about the "BP Oil Spill," also known as, "The Deepwater Horizon Disaster," and how it has affected Pensacola, Florida, as well as the Gulf Coast. It's an account of history that you most likely will never be taught in any public school. To follow the events described in this book, simply go to:

www.youtube.com/user/WoMenHead101

Introduction

The Journey Begins

There's nothing more motivating than a tragedy. And on September 11, 2001, emotions fueled the entire planet into change. Thanks to CNN, the Internet, and other media sources, people around the world were simultaneously feeling the shock and horror, as images of the 9/11 attacks unfolded, on New York's twin towers.

A 2010 psychological study found that text messages sent on the day of the attacks spiked with words identified with anxiety and anger. And researchers discovered something spiritually new that day. The collective influence the human heart has on the planet.

Although science has barely scratched the surface, there is evidence that the changes in the planets magnetic field have an effect on the brain and nervous system. Frequencies found in the Earth's ionosphere correspond to the frequencies of the human heart and brain.

There is actually a scientific study called the Global Coherence Initiative that establishes a monitoring system (GCMS) that measures fluctuations in the magnetic fields generated by the earth and in the ionosphere. GCI researchers theorize that the collective human response to global events can affect the earth's field.

On a personal level, the morning of September 11th, marked the third year anniversary when my life partner, Celia, and I met. We had just returned from a two week vacation in Pensacola, Florida. We brought back a black and tan German shepherd puppy, with a white cross on his chest. He had caught the deadly Parvo virus shortly after we came home. On that morning, I knew he was going to be survivor. So it started out as a good morning.

At 8:45 a.m., when the attacks began, I was in route to an office meeting. It was my third year as a Realtor in Columbus, Ohio. I was just beginning to see a solid income from endless weekends of open houses, and days upon days of walking through residential neighborhoods passing out flyers and post cards. My name was starting to get around, and I was getting referrals.

Shortly after I arrived at the office is when the phone calls began. At first it was an associate's wife calling to tell us what had happened to the first tower. I remember thinking, "Terrorist attack? No way!"

But then a second call came in announcing that the second tower had been hit by a commercial jet. When my associate repeated what his wife had said, I jumped up out of my seat and headed directly home.

When I reached my car and started the engine, the radio blasted information, instead of music. You know something big is up when every radio station in the city stops regular programming to air the news. Fear had already gripped my thoughts, before I had even seen the television.

When I did make it home, I found myself glancing at Celia, as a plane flew above our house, on its way into Port Columbus International. Both our faces fell from the sky and our eyes locked in total disbelief, as our mouths hung open. Soon after that, the planes quit coming.

And through all that, one thing kept nagging at my mind. It was a dream I had two years previous.

Celia and I are walking down a busy city street, when something hits me. I look in the direction from where the object came from and there sits a broken rock on the other side of a chain link fence. We are standing on a street corner, across the street from where the rock fell.

Out of the corner of my eye, I see another huge rock flying our way, out of the sky. It lands in the same place and shatters when it lands. I say to Celia, "Look! They're coming off of that Church and bouncing off the roof of that building."

The church is tall, and the steeple is high in the sky, but there's a fence around it. All of a sudden, more and more rocks are coming from the steeple high in the sky. I run across the street and stand on the corner near the church. Celia and some other people are laying on the ground. I see someone's face that I know, but I can't remember who it was. I'm concerned about their safety, and I wonder why they don't move across the street - out of the way of danger.

One of the things that raced in mind as I watched the television set was that those people have got to move and get out of the way of those towers. Call it intuition or a hunch, what ever, but I knew those towers were going to fall.

Like I said, there's nothing more motivating than a tragedy, and the following year Celia and I sold the house and moved to Florida. When we moved to Pensacola, in 2002, we were surrounded by white crystal sand that used to squeak as bare feet walked upon it.

My first job was with a Catholic Church. I was born and raised Catholic, but was not a Sunday morning attendee. I hadn't participated with a church, since my parents pulled us out of Catholic school, shortly after my mom and dad divorced. It was the early 70's. It wasn't until the mid 1990's that I began to pray steadily, at night before I would feel asleep.

Still, I was hired as a receptionist. I guess having a cousin, who was a priest helped. My duties included researching articles for the Church bulletin, and the layout and design of the newspaper as well. Again, a dream I had in 1999 came into play in a most fascinating way.

I walk out of the bathroom and there's a celebration going on. There's a priest giving a sermon, and handing out palms. Suddenly, my uncle, shown as an old man with grey hair, who looked like Colonel Sanders, shows up. He keeps saying to himself, "I wish everyone would just leave me alone."

I began working for the Church the first part of 2003. The priest I worked for wanted nothing more than to retire and be left alone. 03/03/03, marked the 40th anniversary of my baptism. My uncle, who died in Vietnam in 1968, was listed as my godparent on my baptismal certificate. In the Catholic belief, godparents are responsible for the child's religious education (foundation). Three is the number of the spirit. Four is the number of the physical, or the foundation. Three (the triangle) above four (the square) symbolizes the spirit rising. The numbers three plus four equals seven, representing truth.

Palm Sunday goes hand in hand with Easter (spirit rising). And Palm Sunday symbolizes Jesus' triumph over temptation, after returning from the desert for 40 days and 40 nights.

Church's may serve a purpose, but church's love to put God in a nice little box too. Apparently, I looked too much like the lesbian I am, and therefore I did not fit properly in their God box. But it wasn't until we took a direct hit from Hurricane Ivan, that I was shook freely from the Catholic tree.

Talk about an emotional event. I had never before seen such devastation from a natural disaster. The church grounds were splintered with pine trees everywhere! It was awful; it looked like a bomb went off. It was weeks before you could find any real meat. Hamburger and steaks were night time dreams, fueled by the hum of generators. Even the priest was far from being God like during those initial two weeks. Partners, husbands, and wives split up and moved away. Yet there was a baby boom locally as well. Like I said, tragedy brings about change. Or as Deepak Chopra, M.D. put it, "All great changes are brought on by chaos."

The tree is only as strong as the winds that test it. And humanity now faces the biggest challenge ever - saving life as we know it; saving the water!

One With Water

"Be like water making its way through cracks. Do not be assertive, but adjust to the object, and you shall find a way round or through it. If nothing in you stays rigid, outward things will disclose themselves.

Empty your mind, be formless. Shapeless, like water. If you put water into a cup, it becomes the cup. You put water into a bottle and it becomes the bottle. You put it in a teapot, it becomes the teapot. Now, water can flow or it can crash. Be water my friend." - Bruce Lee

Life evolved from the sea. Not to mention, we were surrounded by water all the way up till the time we left our mothers womb. Water is one of the basic four components needed in order for there to be life. The measure of salt in our blood is the same as what can found in the oceans. Water is believed to be the most receptive of the four elements.

It is also the most mystical.

In the cult classic movie, Donnie Darko, water is the barrier element used as a gateway between universes. The same holds true for the Keanu Reeves film, Constantine, in which Reeves travels between this universe and the underworld. And according to legend, St. Rasputin of Russia, who was a mystic and visionary, also known as the "Mad Monk," after raping a nun among other outrageous behavior, was killed by drowning in December 1916, because it was believed throughout the community that if one was truly a saint, then they could not die by drowning. Rasputin may not have lived a saintly life and died as a consequence of a myth. But still, we know the moon has a direct relationship between human emotions and the ocean tides. And science has recently confirmed this relationship between man and water.

Masaru Emoto, from Japan has published six books (1996-2007) that claims human consciousness has a direct effect on the molecular structure of water. Considering ninety percent of the human body is made up of water, Emoto's research can most certainly prove a direct correlation between the two, which will be discussed more thoroughly later in the book.

And water doesn't just fall fresh out of the sky; it recycles by evaporating, forming clouds, and then returning to the earth in the form of rain. As a result of the Deepwater Horizon disaster, on April 20, 2010, we now know that rain can contain oil and pollutants. Two months after the oil began to spill into the Gulf, residents were reporting that their swimming pools were collecting oil.

Marine biologist, Riki Ott, who happened to be living in Alaska during the Exxon Valdez oil spill, in 1989, had warned people along the Gulf coast to avoid the rain, before she left the area that fall. When she returned to the Gulf, on May 7, 2011, she stated at a conference with the Pensacola League of Women Voters, that she could tell who had been out in the rain, and who hadn't by the sound of their voice. Which just goes to prove even further that what we do to the water, we do to ourselves.

And it's not just the Gulf States that are under attack right now.

Gas and oil companies are performing an operation called hydraulic fracking. Whereas they inject water and sand under high pressure into super deep wells to crack open rocks to release hydrocarbon molecules like oil and natural gas. In order to do this they use corrosion resistant toxic chemicals such as benzene, formaldehyde and many others. Small communities have been destroyed by this senseless act. In some areas where this is conducted, you can turn your water on in the household sink, but be careful if you put a lighter near it, because it will catch on fire. There are even areas of the land where streams and creeks bubble with gas.

Tar Sands is another way these oil and gas companies are raping our Mother Earth. It's like squeezing oil from sand. It is the dirtiest and most unproductive way of to obtain oil. It leaves the land a barren waste and is to be transported though pipelines from Canada, into the United States to be sold to Eastern countries like China. And because sand erodes the pipelines quickly, we set ourselves up for further contamination our land and water. Tar sands are heavy. If a pipeline breaks near the water, it sinks to bottom. There is no known way to clean it up.

Exxon Mobile, who was making five million dollars in profit alone every single hour, twenty-four hours a day, in the first half of 2011, trashed the Yellowstone River in Billings, Montana

To add insult to injury, it's the very same oil and gas tycoons who pollute our water that want to sell us water in a bottle straight from the tap. Privatization of water is the new greed. Blue gold they call it. Even the plastic bottles used to trap this simple tap water are made of oil.

Thanks to Jessie Ventura's, "Conspiracy Theory," we know the Bush family purchased the largest water aquifer in the world. It is part of 100,000 acres they purchased in Paraguay. And another oil man named T-Boone Pickens purchased sixty-eight thousand acres in Northern Texas that lies directly over the largest aquifer in the United States. And in Texas, if the well is under your land, and you can get to it, then it's yours. And 'ole T-Boone has no problem bragging about the money he's making by monopolizing the water supply in the dry west. If he could bag up the air this dude would do it.

Does it not alarm you that oil tycoons are buying up the fresh water sources?

Since the Deepwater Horizon (DWH) exploded, there have been five other oil spills in the United States alone (not including other countries around the world).

35 days after DWH
Anchorage, Alaska. Pipeline Breaks. BP Oil.

52 days after DWH
Salt Lake City, Utah. Red Butte Creek. Pipeline. Chevron.

97 days after DWH
Michigan. The Kalamazoo River. Pipeline. Enbridge.

98 days after DWH
Barataria Bay/Gulf of Mexico, Louisiana. Pipeline. Exxon.

437 days after DWH
Billings, Montana. Yellowstone River. Pipeline. Exxon.

Oil Company strikes again and poisons another public water supply, while buying up land that contains huge aquifers of untainted water. Have I raised your eyebrow yet?

There was a time when I was just a regular girl having fun, with no cares in the world. Then the largest oil disaster the United States had ever seen turned my world upside down, and I found myself fighting for the one thing that gave me my greatest joy - the Gulf of Mexico. This is my story; my truth.

Dream Journal Entry
November 22, 1998

I'm in the desert. I'm trapped here, by two buff cops. They told me I was not allowed to leave this place. I'm on top of a mountain mesmerized by a clean, cool, blue, soothing body of water. It was so inviting. But the two cowboys were now standing in the water with shot guns.

I climbed down from the mountain and asked, "Am I allowed in the water?"

With dark sunglasses and no facial expression, the uniformed men answered, "It wouldn't be a good idea to swim in the water."

All the same, I sensed no danger and took my clothes off. Others started gathering around. Standing naked, I told them that the water was good, and there was nothing to be scared of. It's ok to stand in the water.

I stepped into the water. It was good.

Depending on the dream, you might not have any idea at all what you just envisioned in your mind and felt in your soul, until the day comes when you know it was more than just a dream.

CHAPTER ONE - 2010 Pensacola Beach, Florida

(March)

"Oh my God, there's something in the water! They've done something to the water! I can't believe this shit!"

"Calm down, calm down, there's nothing wrong with the water. It just looks bad from the surf turning up the sand."

As if that thought hadn't crossed my mind after spending every free minute I had on the beach for the past eight years. "No, I'm telling you there's something wrong with the water Celia!"

"No, no, I'm sure it's nothing. You'll see."

What grabbed at my heart that day, I'll never know. Maybe it was a frightened voice from the future trying to warn me? Why not? It wasn't as far-fetched as it sounded. When I was a child, maybe eleven or twelve years old, I came really close to drowning. It was a near death experience that stuck with me through out my life. It pretty much shaped me and molded me into the person I am today. But most importantly the experience taught me that time is irrelevant.

(1974 Delaware, OH) - "Come on, I'll race you!" There was a sign sticking up out of the flooded waters, where we would normally sit, when we visited the beach. "The first one to the sign wins!"

Being the second oldest of the group and very athletic, I was the first to reach the sign. Knowing that the sign was no taller than I, when I reached it, I wearily stepped down. I hadn't realized that the water had washed away the sand that surrounded the sign, and I found myself way over my head in the murky water that had now filled my lungs and taken my breath away.

It's true what they say, you're third time down is the last time. And on my second trip up, I could see my mother sitting on the beach watching. There was no panic in her facial expression at all. But I knew I was in big trouble. After my third time down, my life flashed before my eyes, and a calm come over me just as fast. I was no longer afraid. I saw Jesus standing before me. His arms were outstretched and inviting. There

13

was an angel on each side of him; they were kneeling as if in prayer, as they gazed at Him, with adoring eyes.

Then boom, the vision and all the comfort was gone! The panic did not return though; just a lot of commotion. My older cousin had pulled me from the water. I wasn't unconscious and very much aware of what just happened.

When I think back to that day in Ohio, and how fast my life passed before me, it was like living every moment that ever happened to me, at once. It wasn't linear, like living one day after the other. But like rolled in a ball, and melted together as one experience. The encounter instilled the belief that the person I am today is a consequence of the person I was, as well as the person I will be; one with my future and my past. Like the water. No beginning; no end.

And on the third day of May, in 2010, as I stood on the white crystal beach in Pensacola, Florida, I was stunned at the dead sea life that was already washing up from the Deepwater Horizon explosion that took place on April 20th. It was cloudy on that Sunday afternoon. And a blanket of sadness seemed to cling like the grey clouds in the air. Five days later I would find myself cutting my hair and donating it for hair booms. The last time I would ever swim in the Gulf of Mexico would be Memorial Day Weekend, at the annual Gay & Lesbian Pride celebration on the beach.

And by June 4th, not even a week later, Sam Champion would be reporting for ABC's Good Morning America, when the tar balls began washing up out of the Gulf. There will be no mistaking the oiled sand balls. It would be twenty days later when the heavy black crude would engulf my soul, right along with the entire white crystal coastline and every living creature in its way. Have you ever heard a dolphin cry?

The Emotional Mortality of an Oil Disaster

June 23, 2010 is when the heavy oil hit Pensacola Beach. I did everything I could to avoid the island. The sadness was more than what my heart could bear. Entire pods of dolphins were crying out. You could see and hear them from the shoreline. Never before had I felt so useless, and for the first time, I understood why someone would want to take their own life. A charter boat captain named Allan Cruise shot himself on his boat that week. I like to believe that God forgave him for that one, because I knew God had to be crying too, and Heaven was about to fall from the sky.

Tropical Storm Alex lingered in the Gulf and was not only expected to become a hurricane, but it also threatened to delay capping the leaking well head for at least fourteen days. There was nothing anyone could do to improve the situation. We were all helpless. All we could do was watch our world disappear.

Two days after the heavy oil hit, hundreds of people gathered on Pensacola Beach and protested offshore drilling, by joining hands along the shoreline. The very first "Hands Across the Sand" protest was earlier in the year, in February, before the oil disaster. It was started in the State of Florida, due to the threat of drilling just off shore of the sunshine state. But thanks to the Deepwater Horizon incident, Hands Across the Sand went viral on June 26, through out the world. And for the first time, since June 4, I wiped away the tears from my cheeks and went to the beach to make a stand in the sand.

I was so scared that I would break down again and start crying. I actually had to talk myself strong and dissociate before I arrived that morning. I didn't know what to expect, which helped my mind focus on other things, other than the sadness that consumed my heart. It was my first protest, and I was clueless as to whether the beach would be open or not. After all, it had only been two days ago since I had viewed thick oil splattered through out my TV set. Where did it go? At the time I didn't know. Nor did I care to stick around and find out.

The odor was ungodly that day. The smell of crude hung heavy in the air. While we were protesting, my friend Ginger bent down to pick up a shell and was splashed by a wave. There was oil dispersant stuck to her key chain and small chunks were found in the pockets of her shorts.

As I spied children playing in the toxic water, I couldn't help but wonder what were these parents thinking? There was a lady with two darling little girls playing in the water just in front of us. I was close enough that I could stick my foot out and kick her in the butt. But she wasn't the only one eye-balling her children from the safety of the shore.

There's eight hundred people standing behind you joining hands, there's an oil skimmer no further out than the end of the pier, and two bulldozers are on the beach as well. It was more than evident that the oil was there, but apparently it wasn't going to stop the people from enjoying their vacations. Suddenly, I found myself more worried about my anger, than the anguish in my heart.

Unlike the dream in 1998, when I told people the water was safe and invited them to join me, I found myself creating short little YouTube videos that demonstrated just the opposite. I had always followed my visions to the letter, but I just couldn't in good conscience do it this time. BP poisoned the water with deadly Corexit, as well as the toxic oil. And children were literally playing in the stuff.

YouTube was my way of handling the frustration and releasing the deep sadness I felt in my heart. And that is how WoMenHead101 came to be. Wo-Men Head was actually a code name given to me by an ex-girlfriend, in the mid '90s. When I relocated from Central Ohio to the Bible belt, I began using the name when selling prayer sticks.

So as the salt life became the crude life, Wo-Men Head went from artist to accidental activist. The original logo changed from an angel, hawk and owl, to a black shadow image of Celia and I standing on the beach, with me holding two fingers up as a gesture of peace.

Other changes included withdrawing from friends and family, especially those from up North. I used to jab fun at them up there, because of the beautiful warm and sunny weather we seemed to enjoy endlessly here in Florida. And you know I was the envy of them all, after sending everyone photos, shells and sand from the beach, especially in the winter time. I use to call friends and family once a week and rub it in. I was quite the jolly soul back then. But now, I lived in a waste land. And their questions made salt water fall from my eyes.

Three of my closest friends left Pensacola after the oil spill. And making friends down this way had not been easy. Losing three in one year wasn't too funny either. It wouldn't be until a year later that I would realize that I had lost that part of me that loved to clown around.

Will the Wolf Survive?

Beach businesses were hurting; there was no denying it. The island looked less alive on Independence Day than on a warm Sunday in January. Yet it was still evident that people were visiting the beaches and swimming in the water just by looking at the wooden walk-outs that joined the beach with the smaller parking lots to the East of the main (Casino) beach. There were tar ball stained footprints everywhere! Including those of a child.

There were even signs posted, by the Escambia County Health Department, in the parking lots that put people on Notice that the beach had been impacted by the Deepwater Horizon incident. In short, the signs said avoid wading, swimming, or entering the water and to avoid contact with oil and oily material, especially children and pregnant women. But apparently no one cared.

Then just sixteen days after heavy oil washed up on Pensacola Beach, on Friday morning, July 9th, I about fell over watching WEAR Channel 3.

"The Blue Angels Beach Air Show begins in about an hour, and the Blues will be taking over the skies this afternoon around two, and Jared Willets and Meteorologist, Christian Garman are out there on Pensacola Beach soaking up the sun and enjoying a beautiful day," squawked the newscaster in the studio.

The cameras pan to Jared and Christian standing on the beach, "I'll tell ya, it is a beautiful day but it is a bit - now I'm not a weather man, but it's hot!"

Yeah, It's hot, yeah, and not hard to soak up the sun right now. The huge upside is there's not a cloud in the sky . . ." declared the meteorologist.

"High show," brags Jared Willets like an excited little boy. "Yeah,

yeah, it's gonna be the high show unless there's a dramatic change. And there's not going to be. But it's very high. Ninety degrees now in Pensacola. That's the new number just in. The good news is at Pensacola Beach is not quite as hot, but, but, very warm."

"That's true, and even better news is the over," as Willets stumbled through the words, "the water will be open for swimming on two occasions .. ."

"Yeah," added Garman, as he wagged his tail like puppy that just pleased his master.

I couldn't believe the local news station was advocating for people to come to the beach and go swimming. Willits was wearing a white shirt, and Garman was wearing an off white shirt, and the sand in the background was darker than either one of them.

The following day was the Official Annual Blue Angels Air Show. Apparently BP kicked in some advertising money for the area, and what we thought would be a perfect weekend for the locals to enjoy the show for once, was just as scary as the oil spill itself. People came from everywhere! It was the biggest turn out we had ever seen! Celia and I decided to bypass the slow crawl traffic and drive to Navarre to get onto the island. The only BP workers seen that day were hidden on the Santa Rosa County side of the beach, far from tourist eyes.

It had been rumored twice that week that BP workers were told to only look busy. And as we drove past a large crew, I concluded it had to be true. One person actually was kicking sand up in the air. So we pulled off the road and began video taping. As we shot our video, one worker kept walking in circles, while another simply stood there the entire time doing absolutely nothing, and another was scratching his ass and then bent over and began staring at the sand. These three people stood within fifty feet of each other and were observed for a good two minutes or more.

Celia broke out in a rash, after about twenty minutes on the beach that day, and we left the island immediately. When we arrived home, she showered and the rash disappeared. We were left with the most logical assumption that in had to be something in the air, or something toxic she had touched on the beach. I was a cigarette smoker at the time, and seemed to be totally unaffected by the environment. But I've never been allergic to poison ivy either. We're all different, and people seemed to react a little differently to the chemicals that became part of the atmosphere along the coast. Some would die from chemical exposure, before a year would even pass.

Hear No Evil, See No Evil, Speak No Evil

Wikipedia actually has a page dedicated to, "Denial." The simple definition of denial is the disbelief in the existence or reality of a thing (like oil). Kind of reminds me of that Shaggy song, where he got caught butt naked, banging the girl next door, on the bathroom floor. But he continues to stick to his story, by constantly repeating, "It wasn't me," to his girlfriend, who caught him red handed.

A second type of denial is minimization, where one might admit a fact, but deny the seriousness. The third is a kind of denial where the subject admits both the fact and seriousness of a given situation, but denies the responsibility, called projection. Thus, denial is a negative characteristic.

Addicts are a consequence of denial. It plays an important role in recovery, via the twelve-step program. And the American Heart Association blames the delayed treatment of heart attacks on denial. Furthermore, the first of Elisabeth Kubler-Ross's five stages of grieving is denial; then anger, bargaining, depression and finally acceptance. So you see, even victims are not immune to the disease of denial. I know, because I wanted to believe the oil was gone too.

The majority of the Pensacola population became victims of denial, when they began supporting BP's false allegations regarding the impact the oil was having on the environment. It was like one day I woke up, and I found myself on the wrong end of the gun. Trolls began to attack my character and the content of the videos that I was presenting. The assaults came from faceless YouTube channels dedicated to planting seeds of doubt to anyone watching the truth unfold. I soon found myself, one of two YouTubers left representing Pensacola.

Gregg Hall, a.k.a. "pcolagregg", became quite popular, after video taping the Gulf water boiling at the shoreline, back in June. Whereas I would take a creative approach by mixing music and news once a week, Gregg was out there everyday. He uploaded his video directly from his cell phone, and he wasn't afraid to dig in the sand and expose himself to the toxic oil, introducing it once again into the air. I use to hate watching his videos, because I too wanted to buy into the denial. Plus, it made my stomach turn when I would see the black goo Gregg uncovered. It was something I couldn't get use to seeing.

Still, the Deepwater Horizon well was capped on July 15th, 2010. BP was dumping so much Corexit into the water, the media and the public were scratching their heads asking, "Where is the oil?"

BP responded with, "It's safe to eat the seafood too!" It would be a month before area fishermen began to speak out in regards to recovering oil in Pensacola Bay. On August 29, Kimberly Blair of the Pensacola New Journal reported, ""We were recovering it in a boat . . . scooping it up out of the sand and dumping it into bags. They're just trying to keep it quiet. Out of sight, out of mind," said a commercial fisherman who asked not to be identified, because he was working for BP in the cleanup and feared losing his job." And there were photos to back his words up.

The oil was in the bay including along Bayfront Parkway, Pensacola Pass, Big Lagoon, Old River to Perdido Bay, Santa Rosa Sound, and near shore in the Gulf of Mexico. And at that time, BP reported that at least 175,000 million gallons of dispersants had been used; but scientists doubted BP and doubled that number. It was rumored that low flying planes were still dumping dispersant in the bay under the cover of night. In addition, beach residents were finding traces of oil and other chemicals in their blood, including the relentless Gregg Hall.

If it wasn't for Gregg Hall, we would still have thick sheets of oil buried underneath the tainted sand of what's left of our beaches. Gregg pretty much forced BP into reversing itself a second time in a two day period.

On September 1, Kimberly Blair was on the front page of the

News Journal once again telling readers that BP couldn't dig more than six inches deep into the sand. But nobody knew who, why or what dictated the stupidity of such a law. Not even Buck Lee, Director of the Santa Rosa Island Authority. "We want to find out who the person is that said no," defended Lee.

It wasn't until two days later when WEAR TV presented the public with the lame excuse that digging anymore than six inches into the sand was a violation of the National Historic Preservation Act, stating that only an archeologist could dig further. I found this to be hilarious considering people go to the beach all the time to dig and play in the sand. I'm sure it would be one of the top two answers on Family Feud's, "What do people do when they go to the beach?"

Not to mention, Celia and I both witnessed the beach being refurbished, after we had moved here in 2002. They stuck a boat out in the Gulf about a couple hundred yards out with a long hose. It sucked sand up from the sea floor and shot it up onto the beach. The beach was refurbished before Hurricane Ivan (2004) and again afterwards. The sand on Pensacola Beach gets whipped up every time a good storm comes through the Gulf. Never in the entire time I have lived here has anybody said, "You can't dig more than six inches on the sand."

On September 5, I decided to challenge the insanity of such a notion. So Celia and I took our camera and we dug a hole six inches deep or more to put up an umbrella in the sand. You could hear the wind in the air when we panned the beach and showed how other people were breaking the law by digging in the sand to secure their umbrellas too. One couple appeared to be sneaking off the beach with a bucket and shovel. "How dare they!" I joked.

But on September 20, when a good friend came to visit, it wasn't so funny anymore. Carol had relocated to the Tampa area, right before the Deepwater Horizon blew. She asked about the beach, so we took her out and decided to dig for oil this time. We didn't have to dig deep, and we didn't even have to dig on the shoreline. We were up by the dunes. It wasn't thick oil, like Gregg showed on the western side of the island. It was more like an oil residue. It smelled awful. We buried it back right away. But now the sand was mixed, and my throat became sore. And it stayed that way for few days or so afterwards.

From that moment on, all I could think about was the children. There was no doubt in my mind that the beach was not a safe place for children to be playing. I never thought I'd say this, but it really sucked that the beach looked so beautiful; even the water appeared to be clean and so inviting. But it was all just a facade. Even if you couldn't see oil, it didn't mean that there wasn't any Corexit or some other highly toxic dispersant in the sand. It was all mixed together. Yet, all of those tourists were encouraged to come down and play in the Gulf of Mexico.

The Dilemma of Lisa Nelson

Lisa Nelson was a massage therapist, who lived and worked in Orange Beach, Alabama (approximately thirty miles from downtown Pensacola). During a November 7 (2010) YouTube interview, with Jerry Cope, Lisa said she was out on the beach on the 22nd of September to see the Harvest Moon. When she returned home that night, she said she had a major attack on her throat and head. She said it felt like knives were sticking in her throat and her throat closed up. It was obvious during the interview that she had trouble breathing. Her voice was raspy, and her face and neck were swollen three times the normal size. She had bruising all over her chest, along her diaphragm, and on her sides.

The doctors were clueless when it came to treating Lisa's symptoms. Lisa was convinced that BP was spraying Corexit along the coast that evening, while people were out on the beach, admiring the moon. She went to the doctor five times, before the November 7 interview. Lisa stated that they had her on enough Prednisone to kill a horse; she had two shots; and had been on four different kinds of antibiotics. Although nothing seemed to help Lisa heal, her doctor insisted that the southerly wind off of the Gulf had nothing to do with Lisa's symptoms. The doctor believed it was a type of pneumonia, because three other individuals he had seen the morning after the full moon, had symptoms just as Lisa had. "It's a bug going around she told Lisa."

From that point on, Lisa was pushed from one doctor to another. Steroids seemed to be the only answer the doctors had for her. But they only provided temporary relief, if any at all. Lisa passed away on March 7, 2011. Lisa's death shared headlines with several dolphins washing up dead along the Mississippi and Alabama coast.

The Pope, The Queen & The Economy

On July 30, Kenneth Feinberg told a crowd of Gulf Coast residents on Orange Beach that he was going to simplify the claims process, by eliminating the extra paperwork (that BP continually used as an excuse not to appropriate funds). Feinberg also promised that claims would be paid within three weeks. On September 16, not only had BP continued to ignore the oil buried on the beach, but Feinberg fell short on his promises as well. Only twenty-two percent of claims had been paid, as reported by the Pensacola News Journal.

As I watched the Queen of England rubbing elbows with the Pope on the evening news that very same night, the ABC anchor never once mentioned how British Petroleum (BP) contributed to the lack of employment our nation was facing, as she tackled the topic of the National Economy. I was livid!

How is it we allow a British company to contribute to the destruction of the economy of this nation, when it was that very same empire that prompted America to free herself from the tyranny of the royals, known as the Revolutionary War?

By all rights, British Petroleum shouldn't even be in business anymore. The entire coast line between Louisiana and Northwest Florida should have been evacuated in 2010. There are thousands of Lori Nelson's out there. Every dime of profit BP makes belongs to the people of the Gulf Coast and no one else. Not the CEO, not the Chairman, the Board of Trustees, or any other BP executive. Needless to say, it was never their oil to begin with. It wasn't the shores of England that were splattered dead and black, like a war zone.

In Pensacola, I began to see new faces standing at busy

intersections, with small simple signs saying, "Anything will help." I was seeing women too; not just men anymore. I saw an electrician in my neighborhood one day, with a sign that said, *"I'm Trying To Expand & Grow Not Stay High Or Glow. Homeless & Unemployed Electrician With Tools!!! Need Day Work But Anything Helps."*

I had even seen a priest holding a sign that said, "Help Needed - Starving Families;" the other side read, "Feed the Poor." I stopped and talked to him. He told me he was used to seeing sixteen or so people at the first of the month in need of some sort of assistance, but now they were coming mid-month as well, and the number of people had increased to eighty-five.

You know, when you see a priest and an electrician, with a business card and tools standing under the hot Florida sun, surrounded by concrete, black pavement, and gleaming metal containers spewing exhaust fog everywhere looking for help, then there's a problem. And there was no denying that BP had contributed greatly to the unemployment in the area. Escambia County (Pensacola) ranked the highest in unemployment throughout the Sunshine State. The majority of the BP clean-up crew was from out-of-state.

What made matters even worse was an eighteen year old Hooters Girl getting paid $20,000 with the promise of three more payments by BP, while business owners were calling it quits due to the lack of business and without any compensation at all by BP. The Hooters girl is the daughter of a close friend of mine. She only worked at Hooters four months prior to the oil spill. Her friend and sister-in-law, a year or two older, had only worked at Hooters three months prior to the spill and received approximately forty-five to sixty thousand dollars; she got boob job with her money. Go figure.

Two other women working at an Applebee's, on Nine Mile Rd, in North Pensacola, made claims with BP and were paid too. They do not own any property on the beach. They lived nowhere near the beach, and their place of employment was approximately thirty miles north of the beach. But they got paid, while doors closed for those who truly needed the money. And that's your twenty-one percent of claims paid, since

Feinberg had taken over the claims process.

Truth and Consequences

Being a minority isn't easy by any means. Celia wasn't crazy about participating in the videos we shot of the beach. She wanted to deny the oil was there along with everyone else. But I kept after her, as if I was trying to convince myself. I relied on her to keep me grounded, and my imagination in check. Plus, including Celia in the videos seemed to keep the trolls away. A second set of eyes gave our presentation more credibility.

Still, when everybody wants you to shut up, they tend to sling crap at you. One day when Celia and I were crossing over to the island, the guy at the toll booth called me "Injun Joe," (Injun Joe was a character in the Adventures of Tom Sawyer; he was an Indian who was portrayed as evil) and he made a couple other smart Alec remarks, before he allowed us to cross the toll booth. And twice I'm sure we were followed, while we were on the island.

By mid October BP let their guard down and began to tackle the buried oil on the beach. Considering it was a step in the right direction, I let my guard down as well. They made quite a show of it. There was heavy equipment everywhere. And tourist were far and few in between during the fall and winter months.

On the morning of October 22, on my way to work, I felt compelled to do a video about why I felt dedicated to do the videos. I didn't want to be at war with my community. I wanted to tell my story. I edited the video that evening when I got home, and posted it the next morning on YouTube. My video not only explained why I continued to post videos of the beach, but it gave props to Gregg Hall and a handful of other people I knew of that supported the cause. The same day I posted the video, Gregg Hall decided to call it quits. He deleted his YouTube channel completely, as well as his facebook page. I sometimes wondered if he would have seen my video first, maybe he would have never erased all that history regarding the oil spill. It was such a loss.

Word was that Gregg was tired of the harassment. I found out a week or so later that he had lost his job, as well as his truck. Southern men in this area have a hard on for their pretty white pick-up trucks. Needless to say, Gregg hit his breaking point. I had been threatened a couple of times on YouTube, and I figured with Gregg putting six times more the video out there than I, he probably received at least three times the amount of threats as I did, if not more. And truth be told, when you're faced with negative circumstances day after day, it works on your nerves, regardless of who you are. Gregg lived on the beach and had to deal with oil in his front yard daily. Not to mention the health issues he had to confront as well. On October 26, Gregg started a new YouTube channel, called True Reporting. But he never did another video regarding the oil on Pensacola Beach, after November 30th.

My employer had been throwing threats my way since the first of August. I guess that's when they decided I wasn't good for business anymore. On November 15th, I lost my job.

I was working for a real estate company, as a rental property inspector. I was glad when they cut me loose. I had become tired of fighting endless faces of ignorance and greed. I couldn't say that I lost my job, because of the oil spill, but I soon found out that WoMenHead101 was going to keep me out of the real estate profession, as long as I kept producing videos showing the oil on the beach, and toxic dispersants, like Corexit, in the water. I may not have been using my real name on YouTube, but my face apparently made its rounds within the community.

Still, I had come this far, and someone had to speak and represent those who couldn't represent themselves. And throughout the rest of the month, I shot video and told the story that no one else wanted to. Thousands of tar balls began washing up out of the Gulf along Pensacola Beach. It was rumored that there were tar balls as big as my feet washing in on Johnson's Beach, approximately eleven miles away.

It cost eight dollars to get onto Johnson's Beach, which is part of the Gulf Islands National Seashore, in Perdido Key. It was littered with so many tar balls that it made it hard not to step on one. I was not surprised to see families playing in the sand and water. Celia and I had gotten pretty used to the stupidity by this point in the game. But I was amazed at how someone would want to pay eight dollars to play in that brown sticky stuff that looked like dog feces, when they could have gone swimming elsewhere for free.

Thousands of man-o-wars began to wash up later in the month of November, for the second time since the spill. I had photos of the creatures before the oil spill hit, and when I went to match them with the man-o-wars that were washing up, they looked sickly in comparison. And there seemed to be an awful lot of black where there should have been blue. In the eight years I had lived here, I had never seen so many jelly fish and man-o-wars wash up on the beach like I did that fall.

The last video Celia and I put out, for 2010, was on November 21. Like Gregg, I was ready for a break. It was the holiday season. The season of love, and peace on Earth and goodwill towards man and all those cozy emotions that were missing in my life; yet very much needed.

Celia and I began arguing half the time when we went out to do the oil videos anyway. "What's that smell like to you?" I'd ask.

"I don't know? Exhaust fumes from one of the boats out there I guess."

"What boat?" I asked.

"I don't know? There's a boat way out there," Celia argued.

"I don't see a boat. What are you talking about?"

"I don't know, but I know there's a boat out there somewhere!"

"You know, you don't have to get pissed off with me Celia! I'm not the one who spilled oil all over the freaking beach! If you want to get mad at somebody, get mad at BP and tell it like it is! It smells like oil!"

"Get that camera off me now!" Celia snapped back.

After a while, you begin to question yourself. Am I being obsessive over this oil spill or what? The only support I found was in a handful of YouTube comments that supporters posted in response to our videos. At the time, I truly believed that I wasn't going to do anymore videos of the beach again. Plus, BP was going to clean the oil up. "They said so."

It wasn't until the holidays that I realized how depressed I had become. I found myself wanting to go back to Ohio. I missed my family and friends. And I knew Celia did too. She had three grandchildren now. The third just came to us in October. But the Northern wind reminded me of how cold it can get up there. And I chased away the thought with a shiver.

"How would you feel about moving to Tennessee?" I suggested.

"It snows up there too. Why can't we just go back to Ohio?" Celia begged, yet adding, "I don't want move. I like my job, and I like the people I work with."

And that's exactly how it feels when you become unsure of yourself. It was like being pulled into two different directions. Should I stay or should I go? Is that crude I smell coming off the water, or is it fumes from some far away ship? Do I have the flu? Or is my body reacting to the oil and dispersants in my blood? Is it safe to live here anymore? Am I crazy? Did the toxic air eat away at my brain cells? Maybe cigarettes saved me, and the air took away everyone else's intelligence? Maybe I'm not crazy after all - they are!

Dream Journal Entry

December 5, 1998

  Someone suggest that we go the beach. Celia and I are sitting in the sand. The sun is warm and the water just reaches our feet on the beach. Someone wants to leave, but I'm like, "not yet, the sun feels good." I stay, and they go back to the hotel.

  Some big dark dude comes along, and he's handing our different hats. Each hat represents a responsibility. He gives me a yellow hard hat that says supervisor on it. I tell him I don't want it, but he's a jolly fellow, and he insists that I take it.

  I think my responsibility had something to do with coordinating lunch. The dude leads me to a tented room on the beach, where we are about to eat. Everybody helps prepare the table.

CHAPTER TWO – The Rapture

2011 started out like a sci-fi novel with hundreds of birds falling out of the sky, in Arkansas. Then it happened in Texas, and other areas of the country began to report the same phenomena. Here on the Gulf Coast, it was dead baby dolphins that began washing up on shore. Mostly in Louisiana and Mississippi, but eventually one washed up in Alabama, and another unreported on Navarre Beach, in Florida. And that's not counting the other dead wildlife that washed up daily, hidden by BP, who cleaned the shoreline at the crack of dawn.

Everyone wants the dead stuff kept hush, hush. Bad for business you know. One day I stumbled onto a trash bag of something dead, but I couldn't open it. I just didn't have the stomach for it. Between the odor, and the maggots in the sand, I was totally disgusted.

Spring time came and so did a melt down of three nuclear reactors in Japan. Now, not only was the Gulf poisoned, but the Pacific Ocean no longer had much to offer in enjoyment either. Seafood was no longer an option. The chances of getting fresh fish without it being tainted slimed extremely. The salt life was rapidly falling out of fashion. And the crude reality of my Pensacola home became more of curse instead of a blessing. Although I did begin to meet some new online friends through Facebook, thanks to a fresh YouTuber representing the Pensacola area. But I soon discovered that my new support system was adding to the doom and gloom as well.

Everyday there was new information regarding the oil spill along the Gulf Coast, including a stream of never ending visuals of dead sea turtles, and various birds playing in brown foamy water along the shoreline. The ill stricken beaches of contaminated sand reminded me of an old lady's vein clotted leg. I found myself submerged in dark depression. My environment was sad and dying. I had to change it.

I gave up smoking cigarettes at Lent, because I figured if it made me healthier, maybe my sacrifice would reflect on the Gulf, and she would heal as well. In the past year, I had come to link the two as one - the smoking and the oil spill. A part of me blamed myself for the oil spill coming upon our shores. I held closely to my belief that what you put out there is what comes back to you. It had to be something I did or I didn't do to cause this oil spill to happen.

I needed to heal. I had to find a way to get my feet back to the Earth. On average, American's spend ninety-five percent of their lives indoors. That's why so many people live in a depressed condition. I was no longer swimming with the manta rays, dolphins, sea turtles, and the little toe biting fish that we named, "Damits." These were the things that made me smile. Rolling in the waves like a child is tickled, while soft white caps riding the clear emerald green water brushed my cheeks, with salt water kisses. I had to get back to the basics. Since it wasn't safe to swim in the Gulf, Celia and I started a little garden; partially out of fear that the economy here in the United States was going to collapse. Yet the main focus was on getting our hands in the dirt and returning back to nature. But what really helped was a good old fashion road trip back home.

Marion, Ohio was a days journey from Pensacola; approximately a thirteen hour drive. The day before I left Florida, tornados ripped across Alabama, killing over three-hundred and fifty people. The aftermath was evident as I traveled I-65 North. Broken trees laid along the side of the road. Four hours into the drive, I seen towering metal light post bent in half along the Birmingham freeway. One post was ripped from the ground and resembled a twisted piece of art on display for all to see. And by the time I reached the Tennessee boarder, I could smell the earth. An aroma I had forgotten; it had been so long.

I hadn't been home for over two years. Normally it would have been a party, but I just couldn't feel it. My hometown was looking rough. They hadn't seen the sun shine for over forty days. Parts of the county were flooded. The roads throughout the city were full of potholes, with some roads even closed. Abandoned buildings, like ghost from business past, littered the small town. The end of the world was here for sure. As I took a look around, I realized how lucky I was to be living in Florida. At least we had the sunshine. It was the first of May, and I had to wear jeans to stay warm throughout my visit in Ohio.

The only constant I could find within this town was the railroad. The city of Marion was basically built upon the steel industry and the railway. When I was a kid, it was the Erie- Lackawanna Railroad. Today it's the rail center for CSX and Norfolk Southern. The names may of changed, but the tracks were still the same. The tracks that my family helped lay across the land. And it was there that I heard the spirits of my relatives calling out to me. I was reminded of who I was, and the importance of the path I had chosen. And when I returned to Florida it was with a renewed sense of purpose.

There had to be something more I could do to help the Gulf, and the people within my community, other than videotaping tar balls in the sand.

I had just started teaching computer classes to one of my old metaphysic's instructors, before I had left for Ohio. I was happy that our paths had crossed again.

Maia Rizzi was slender with long blonde curly hair and brown eyes. Her face had been graced by an earthly wisdom that reminded me of a soft forest wood; reflective of her Peruvian heritage. She had traveled the globe extensively and carried herself with an air of culture. Maia also held a master's in psychology.

I'll never forget the first time I met Maia in 2007. She was teaching a course called, Creative Visualization. I was kind of nervous about the class, since the lady who owned the store that oversaw the curriculum talked to dead people. Like John Edwards on Sci-Fi.

"Excuse me, I have a quick question about this evenings class," as I looked the store owner dead in the eye, "this class wouldn't have anything to do with, like you know, changing yourself into an animal and moving about the place, or anything like that would it?" I awkwardly asked with a smile.

"No, it does not," the store owner replied sternly.

Hmmm . . . I guess I'm not going to get a smiley face for the day,

"And which way is the classroom?"

When I arrived, Maia was seated by the door. "Hi, I'm Maia. I'll be your Creative Visualization Instructor . . ." as she spoke, I sized her up and wondered if she spoke to dead people too?

And before the afternoon's class was over, Maia had no problem telling me what a judgmental asshole I was. Her honesty intrigued me. She was right. I was just as judgmental as those bible thumpers choking at the collar on a hot summer's day. Waiving a bible from a street corner, while screaming what a sinner I am. Maia pretty much had my attention from that point on. I continued with her classes for the next two years. I valued her opinion highly and learned much regarding the power of thought.

One day we decided to skip computer class and do lunch instead. I shared my fear with her regarding the oil spill and how it came about. "What did I do to bring about this oil spill into my life? You taught me that our thoughts are reflected in our world; what we put out there, we get in return. What did I do to make this spill happen?"

Maia thought about it for a minute, and then she said, "It's the collective."

Kind of sounds like a horror movie doesn't it? "The Collective!" Or maybe I heard it on Star Trek before. I had to ask, "What do you mean by the collective?"

"Collectively, we as a whole people are greedy."

Right away I lit up, "But I'm not greedy! I don't ask for much." Life has taught me, the less you have the freer you are. I haven't used a credit card in years. It cost too much money. Why pay to use your money?

And for me, freedom is what this life's journeys all about. Free to enjoy the Earth as God intended. When I swam and played in the Gulf, I felt free. Free of all my worries. Yes, I know somewhere deep down inside there is some other sort of greed that I feed. Like my greed to enjoy the company of close friends, eating good food, and laughing a lot.

More concerned with my own personal loss, I was still clueless as to what Maia was trying to explain. To help me understand, she turned me onto this book called, "The Biology of Belief," by Bruce Lipton, Ph.D.

Lipton writes in his book about the story of evolution and how in the first three billion years there were only single cell organisms. In order to get smarter and increase awareness, the cells began to group together and formed multi-cellular communities in which they shared awareness. In turn, Lipton applied that knowledge to the human being, which is a huge communion of individual cells who have specific responsibilities. Not only does this science reflect upon humanity and how we individually contribute to a community, or even within the family unit, it also demonstrates that collectively we are far more efficient than as individuals.

Take for instance an assembly line in a factory. When I was much younger I used to work for Whirlpool in Marion, Ohio. The company has been a cornerstone of employment for the small town since I had been born to this world. My uncle worked there, my mom was next, then my aunt got a job there. I eventually found myself working there with at least three of my cousins. And when I relocated to Southern California, my brother found a job with Whirlpool. The Marion Division is notorious for building clothes dryers, including Sears Kenmore, and Maytag.

Assembly lines consist of several people with one mission in mind. And that is to build, on average, twenty-three hundred dryers in an eight hour shift, per line. Now imagine trying to assemble a dryer by yourself from raw material. It would be a matter of days for you to build one clothes dryer by yourself. When we work together collectively, we are far more efficient than working individually by ourselves. And if we continue to follow a pattern of individualism, we will most likely die in contrast to evolving. Kind of like a human shedding dead skin cells.

Nine Eleven and the Deepwater Horizon explosion are triggers calling humanity (the collective) to reevaluate our belief systems. And in 2011, it was happening all over the globe. Dead birds falling from the sky, nuclear melt downs, tornados, earth quakes, hurricanes, floods, the financial market and more oil spills. We as a people are changing; we're evolving. Our beliefs and values are changing.

Before the summer was over, Maia gave me a second book to read called, "The Celestine Prophecy," by James Redfield. It's an adventurous and spiritual story regarding the evolution of mankind. The book describes one of the first indications of this great shift in evolution as a time when people will demand an end to that activity that threatens to harm the nature and beauty of our Earth Mother. That time is now.

What's really awesome is that, "The Biology of Belief," bridges the gap between science and spirituality. And both books reinforce the significance of the power of the human mind.

The Strength of Conviction

Thought is a vital creative force that moves. It is infectious, and it changes rapidly. Sometimes it can be hard to keep up with your thoughts, because they move so fast. The body is a product of the mind. Good positive thoughts can keep you healthy, and bad negative thoughts will bring you sickness and disease.

In his book, "The Biology of Belief," Lipton (at page 112-113) gives an example of how the nocebo effect (opposite of the placebo effect; thinking you have a disease when you don't) can feed into an unjustified belief. In 1974, Nashville physician, Clifton Meador, had a patient named Sam Londe, who was a retired salesman with esophagus cancer. The disease back at that time was considered fatal. Londe ended up dying about three weeks later, to no ones surprise. The surprise came after Londe's death, at which time the autopsy found a small amount of cancer in Londe's body; there was a spot on his lung and one or two on his liver, but not enough to kill him. Most importantly though, there was no esophagus cancer. Not a trace. Three decades later, and Dr. Meador is still haunted by Londe's death. Meador told the Discovery Channel, "He died with cancer, but not from cancer. I thought he had cancer, he thought he had cancer, everyone around him thought he had cancer. . . did I remove hope in some way?"

And here's an example of Lipton's work (at page 109) that goes to prove that the placebo effect doesn't only apply to pills. Published in the New England Journal of Medicine, in 2002, a study lead by Dr. Bruce

Moseley, of Baylor School of Medicine, in which Moseley divided his knee surgery patients into three groups. In the first group, Moseley shaved the damage cartilage in the knee. The second group, Moseley simply flushed out the knee joint. And in the third group, he conducted a fake surgery. The "fake surgery" patients were sedated, the standard incisions were made, he splashed water to stimulate the sound of the knee washing and talked and acted like he would, if he had truly done the surgery. All three groups were given the same post surgery instructions. And guess what?

The placebo group improved right along with first two groups. This study was prompted by the question of which surgery was actually giving Moseley's patients the most relief from their pain. Lipton quotes Moseley as saying, "My skill as a surgeon had no benefit on these patients. The entire benefit of surgery for osteoarthritis of the knee was the placebo effect."

I'm sure by now, you're wondering why it is so very few doctors are stepping up to the plate to share this information with you. "Greed." It begins at the top with the insurance companies, and the pharmaceutical companies, and then it works downward the individual doctors, who lead the medical profession. You figure a doctor performs 2,900 surgeries yearly on knees, at $5,000 each, that's an income well over a million dollars per year.

The trillion dollar per year pharmaceutical industry to this day keeps lobbying Congress to pass laws in an attempt to band natural remedies from being sold over the counter, and further their agenda by purchasing time on national television to convince you that you need a pill for whatever ails you, including depression. When truth be told, you need only to change your environment and your conscious thoughts, instead feeding more negative energy into that depression and taking a drug that can quite possibly kill you.

The drug companies want you to be scared and plant fear of disease in the mind. In being fearful, you compromise your intelligence, as well as your health.

I'll never forget the first time I was asked by one of my new activist friends what my symptoms were. I was like, "What? What do you mean?"

She says, "You know, from the oil the spill?"

It kind of blew my mind, because I never thought of myself as ill. Still I thought back to the few occasions when we did question our health, "Well, one time Celia broke out in a rash, when we were on the beach. Another time, I was digging a hole in the sand and within minutes, I had a sore throat that lasted three days to a week. And one time in August, I was traveling through Alabama and came down with a horrendous sore throat that went away by the time I hit the Northeastern corner of the state. But other than that, neither Celia nor I are sick."

Afraid of offending my new friend, I went on to explain further that I also began the habit of eating a clove of garlic with a glass of red wine in the fall of 2010. I was in the custom of taking Chlorella too. Chlorella is an emerald algae that grows in fresh water. As a supplement it contains all of the B vitamins, plus C and E, as well as major minerals like zinc and iron. It makes for a great detox. And it boosts the immune system, accelerates the healing process and protects against radiation, among other things.

After sharing my success for good health in a blog in March, the word "Detox" began to circulate among the various Facebook groups. And on May 7th, Dr. Deborah D Viglione, M.D., of Gulf Breeze told the League of Woman Voters of Pensacola, "Those toxins right now are going into our fat. And our body does not want us to burn that fat, because it re-exposes us to the toxins. It also goes in our organs and causes all these illnesses. And believe me, I've seen every one of these things she's talking about . . .," as she pointed to the guest speaker, Dr. Riki Ott, ". . . in mass, you know, for the last probably six to eight months. But, myself have been in the sauna eight times. Yesterday afternoon, I started to pee orange urine, and I had this horrible odor come out of my body. Now I realize what it was . . ." as she pointed to Dr. Ott, a second time ". . . but, you know, I thought I hadn't been in the water that much. I try to stay away from the seafood, you know. This is a real, a real big problem, so I'm going to try to organize something in this community, because we need to make everybody aware of, and get help for people, and get other physicians on board."

And Dr. Viglione wasn't the only one hip on detoxification. A registered nurse in the Florida area was offering to help victims of the BP flu, by advising them on how to detox. Which turned out to be more of an comfort than the average traditional doctor who was clueless on how to treat chemical illnesses.

Considering the Gulf of Mexico provides a living environment, much like the human body there is no reason why she can not detoxify as well.

Bioremediation is the process of using microorganisms to remove toxins and pollutants, whereas natural occurring good bacteria is introduced to an affected area of the Gulf to clean the oil and toxins in the water. It's a proven quick acting effective technology as well. It has been around for over thirty years, and it has been used in twenty countries. It works on the surface and in the water column as well. And it's cheap. But our bureaucratic government has not gotten around to approving its use in the Gulf of Mexico (yet).

But that didn't stop a small group of us from concentrating our efforts to heal the Gulf waters. Back in 2007, Maia had introduced a book to the class that was written by a Japanese entrepreneur named, Masaru Emoto. Emoto wanted to test the power that thought and words had on water. So he taped words onto glass containers, so that the word could be read by the water inside. The water would respond to words like, love and gratitude, by crystallizing shiny and white, like snowflakes. But words like hate or even the name Hitler crystallize in somewhat shapeless and unattractive forms.

Considering the human body is made up of ninety percent water, Emoto's experiments may prove that what we say and think has a profound effect on us physically. And to further this theory that thought can clean and heal polluted water, a demonstration of few hundred people, led by a Buddhist Monk, gathered around a polluted stream in Japan and focused on the water healing for an hour. Fifteen minutes after the meditation, it was reported that the water became visibly clearer.

Knowing how concerned and involved I was with the Gulf of

Mexico, Maia gathered six or seven of us together and we began to meet once a month within three days of a full moon. We each collected a small jar of water and would meditate on it until we would meet again the following month. At that time we would say a few words and return the water to the Gulf.

Thought is the water of life, and we live in a vast ocean of thought.

Saved by Water

"Let's get a swimming pool. What do you think?"

"I don't know? I don't think I've met anyone yet who has a pool and doesn't complain about all the time and money they invest in it?" I hastily whined.

"Well, it isn't like we'll be swimming in the Gulf of Mexico this year," Celia snapped back.

She did have a point, "How much are they?"

"They have one at Wal-Mart for two-hundred and fifty dollars. It's three and a half foot deep, by sixteen feet."

"I don't' want to swim in some tiny pool. If we're going to do it, let's go all the way and do it right. What about a five foot pool? How much would that cost?"

"Around five hundred dollars."

As I stood staring at the picture on the box, at Wal-Mart only moments after our conversation, I began to rethink my choice in pool sizes. The box that contained the five foot pool, was enormous. I'm sure they had to use a fork lift to get in on the shelf. "Hey babe, maybe we ought to go with the smaller size and see how it goes? What do you think?"

She must of been feeling overwhelmed as well, because she didn't hesitate to agree.

Snapping out of a depression isn't easy. And it isn't done in a day.

You have to make changes in your life. And when you have no power over the circumstances you find yourself in, you have to make the best of a bad situation. When I returned from Ohio in May I had to agree with Celia that a swimming pool was a good start to changing our environment. We bought a new smoker grill too. We turned our backyard into our own exotic private island. I would wake up in the morning and roll out of bed and into the backyard. My laundry now consisted of mainly swimming shorts and sports bras. I had to remind myself to take a shower because otherwise, why bother? I was just going to wind up in the pool anyhow.

I was collecting unemployment. I made job contacts via Internet and fax machine. I rarely left the house. I saved a butt load of money on gasoline. And I was saving hand over fist from the cigarettes I gave up for Lent. With the party on in the back yard, there was no need for bars or restaurants - its summer time, and we had the king of grills to play with. We traded shrimp and crab legs for slow smokin' ribs, with our own fresh garden foods; mostly tomatoes and potatoes.

Our pool was surrounded by two live oak trees that stretched beyond a Halloween imagination cloaked in hanging vines, where a mocking bird nest dangled in the wind. The trees shaded us and kept the water cool. And mowing the grass was no longer such a chore knowing there was a wet and refreshing treat waiting for when the job was completed.

Instead of playing with little yellow schools of salt water fish, we now were entertained by fluorescent dragon flies dancing upon the sunlight, or an occasional honey bee in need of rescue from the wet water. For only being three and a half feet deep the pool brought us much happiness. Who would of ever of known that something so small and simple would be such good medicine?

Wash me clean . . . release me to be free. I could float for hours looking at the sky. Sometimes the squirrels would play in the tree branches above us. One day, we heard this thump and looked over just in time to see a squirrel jetting for the tree trunk in an attempt to out run our two dogs. Luckily the squirrel beat the dogs up the tree, and Celia and

I had a good laugh.

The squirrels continued to tease and taunt each other, then "Thump!" Another squirrel fell to the ground. I was just happy they didn't fall into the pool while amusing us; otherwise, Celia and I would have become the entertainment.

And I never realized how comforting the sounds of lawn mowers and the clamor of the trash man's truck could be. The summer sounds reminded me of younger days, when I was child day dreaming under the maple tree in my mom's backyard. As my body relaxed and became one with the water, I floated to wherever the water took me, leaving my troubles far behind.

But at no moment did I ever forget about the Gulf. I love the water. When I look out in the Gulf of Mexico I say, "that's my soul out there." I miss her. When I'm by myself in the pool, I tell the water how much I love her, as my thoughts always return to the Gulf. Thought is everything.

So when I found myself with a bad ear infection, I questioned what it was that I was not hearing? So I listened hard. But the other ear began to hurt, even though I had been avoiding the pool (as well as the beach). Then I realized that it was a matter of balance; the balance of philosophy and reality.

There are always outside energies that influence our environment. The water pushes the sand and changes the landscape of the beach every second of every minute throughout the day. The location of the sand bars change. Empty sea shells journey to dry sandy beaches along the shoreline. There is force that molds us and steers us where need be. No one can escape the reality of their destiny. Not even in thought. I realized that I couldn't avoid my responsibility to Mother Earth hiding in my backyard in a swimming pool all summer long; that very same pool that inspired me to tell you this story.

The Fight For Independence

June brought about the third Hands Across the Sand demonstration. It was my second protest. And it was considerably lame compared to the year before, right after the heavy oil had washed up on Pensacola Beach.

Casino Beach was packed with tourists. I spent the first hour wearing a poster board sign that said, "Hell No You Can't Drill Here! And Don't Ask Again!" I stopped people and told them of the demonstration that would be taking place shortly. Some people acted as if I was a vagrant asking for money or something.

I decided to video tape the protest from the pier near by, so I could get a total view of the people joining hands. There were more people sitting on the beach and playing in the water than there were demonstrating. And it was a peaceful demonstration. You simply stand and join hands for fifteen minutes quietly along the shoreline sending out good thoughts. Instead tourists were cutting through the line to get to the water, as if we were an inconvenience to them. I saw one kid kicking sand at a camera man. There was a break in the line at one point, where a guy just flat out refused to hold hands with the guy beside him. And the entire time there is as far as the eye could see, a line of foam floating on top of the water slowly moving towards the people playing along the shoreline.

There were three of us on the pier and we all decided it wasn't natural. All three of us were networked through Facebook with environmental groups who often spoke about Corexit floating on the water; especially on hot days. And that day was no exception to the heat of a blazing southern sun at high noon.

Corexit is a toxic oil dispersant used by BP to sink the oil to the bottom of the ocean, where it stays hidden. It is just as deadly, if not more harmful to the ocean than the oil itself. And it's made by a company that goes by the name NALCO. In 1994, NALCO and Exxon Mobile merged into NALCO Exxon Energy Chemicals.

"You know what? Every state in the United States, except eleven states signed up for Hands Across the Sand. Eleven didn't!" Trisha Williams said as we stared out upon the water. Trisha also photographed the demonstration and was the fresh new YouTuber from the Pensacola area who hooked me up with the local environmentalist.

"Look at that crap in the water, look. Look at it! It's going all up in there where those people are swimming."

"Yeah, that's what I'm video taping right now," I replied.

"It's disgusting!" Trisha professed in a southern bell fashion that is native to most of those born to this part of the United States. She made the word disgusting sound cute.

When we left the pier and came up on the beach Trisha pointed down at the brown and black streaked sand along the shoreline, "See this, right here!"

And no kidding, I'm video taping at this very moment, and some kid actually stretches to grab what appears to be a tar ball washing up. "This is a nightmare for me," Trisha continued.

But when it came to lighting a fire under these people, who complained throughout the days, weeks, and months about the oil spill, it seemed almost impossible to get anyone to demonstrate their concerns.

Hands was on June 25th, and on July 2nd, the Florida Power Ball drawing was to take place on Pensacola Beach. It aired in thirty-three states. It was a perfect opportunity to demonstrate and maybe get some kind of national exposure. Something that had happened only twice since the first of the year thanks to NBC Nightly News reporting on the dead dolphins that continued to wash up on the beach.

So I posted the information on the various Facebook groups and suggested demonstrating. The only comment I got was, "Make sure you get me a ticket while you're there."

There's over two thousand people combined in these Facebook groups that are dedicated to the Gulf. I voiced my frustration to the environmental community, via blog; right after the holiday weekend was over. I asked, "Where is the fire and the passion?"

I wrote, "For living in an area representative of fire, after all, we are the sunshine state, I have to ask, where is the emotion?"

And I finished it with, "Happy Holiday America!" Because face it, it wasn't just the Gulf Coast that seemed to be sluggish, the entire United States had been doing nothing all year.

It wasn't until one month later that three people out of a small group of protesters were arrested in front of BP's offices in New Orleans, Louisiana. Once again Cherri Foytlin had gained my highest respect. She was one of them. As soon as I heard the news on Facebook, I left the comment, "That's what I'm talking about!"

The first time I met Cherri was on March 19, 2011. A mother of six, and she was marching from New Orleans to D.C. in order to bring awareness to the problems we were still facing on the Gulf coast in regards to the oil spill. I was so impressed with her sacrifice that I wanted to give her a prayer stick I had made for the Gulf. It was tall enough to use as a walking stick, and I had been deliberating on what to do with it. Normally I would have left it on the beach, but BP was cleaning the sand. And I didn't want it to wind up in the hands of a BP worker.

So Celia and I got up early on a Saturday morning and hooked up with Cherri and the crew just north of Huxford, Alabama at about 6:30 a.m. It was day seven of Cherri's adventure. And she was already on the road traveling with Drew Landry and Project Gulf Coast. I was surprised at how shy and modest Cherri was when I gave her our gift.

The stick was made of cedar and had images of sea creatures burned into the wood. It was colorfully painted reflecting the joy of the underwater community. I tied white and grey feathers from the beach at the top, and the bright animated feathers of the parrot towards the bottom. I carved out the four faces of the four directions as well at the bottom of the stick.

Right after I gave Cherri the stick we began to walk and just a few yards ahead of where I gave Cherri the gift, we came across a small Indian cemetery belonging to the Poarch Creek tribe. After we stopped and paid our respects we continued to walk, and Cherri and the others told us of the magic they had seen along the way. The road we walked was pretty much deserted and eventually turned into clay in some areas. The scenery could only be described as heavenly. A small group of little birds danced above us as we passed a farm that would fit picture perfect on a postcard.

Even White Bison's Elder's Meditation for the day

45

(www.whitebison.org) addressed a deep wound in the people and a need to get back to the Earth. It spoke of how a feeling of death can devour an entire community. It is a time to reconnect to Mother Earth, and a time of prayer. And as it turned out, I never prayed so much in my life, as I had in 2011.

The Red Road

Jesus said, "Show me the stone that the builders rejected: that is the keystone," from the lost Gospel of Thomas, at 1:66.

The indigenous people of the world have always had a connection to the Earth that conventional religions exclude. Even the mighty Catholic Church, who has always felt the need to bully their beliefs onto these people of a simple and gentle race, has never embraced the concepts of the first people of this nation.

Yet the Christians and most Native American tribes have their similarities. Both have told of prophecies regarding the "The end of times" also referred to as "The rapture". The word rapture is commonly used among American evangelists. By definition it is the transporting or the state of being transported, from one place (Earth) to another (Heaven).

The story "The Celestine Prophecy" takes place in Peru, and it speaks of this time when humanity will evolve spiritually and basically disappear. But it isn't because God simply picked a few good people and left the rest behind. It's because some of us will evolve on a spiritual level to the point where we learn to increase our energy levels and become invisible to those who are still vibrating on a lower level. Kind of like the resurrection of Jesus - where did the body go?

In other words, we learn to cross between this earthly life and the other side, which some call Heaven, in our same form; our human bodies. "On Earth as in Heaven," so to speak. Take for example the Mayan culture. Where did they disappear to?

The Mayan's were known for their mathematical and astronomical techniques. It is the Mayan calendar that predicts the 2012 apocalypse, actually narrowing the date to December 21. No one has ever been able to explain the collapse of this ancient civilization, other than guessing.

Overpopulation? Revolt? Maybe the collapse of trade resources (monetary/economy)? Or maybe an environmental disaster of some kind? Sounds a little familiar doesn't it? These are the same issues that humanity is faced with today.

The Hopi tribe of North America prophesies the end of days as well. "Warriors of the Rainbow," will be a new tribe that will consist of many colors and creeds. They will gather from the four directions, and they will put action above words. They will reach out and teach the others the way of the Creator, and in doing so, they will face much adversity. Still, there will be those who listen to their words and choose to walk with them along this path to the return of innocence. They will rise from the ash of the earth like the thunderbird. And they will lead us to a new reality, restoring balance and harmony to our Mother - Earth.

The Lakota Indians have a similar story as well. According to the Lakota elder, David Swallow, one prophecy originated from a vision quest that Crazy Horse had. On the third day of his quest, he said he heard the voices of children crying out. Then he saw a flash of light in the sky. And they become brighter than day. Then ashes fell from the sky and covered the Earth. The next day the grass was green and the waters were clean. And on this new day, Crazy Horse said he only saw God's children playing upon the Earth.

There is truth in all religions and creeds. People need to become aware and come together and be one mind. We've become a society that is based on consumption driven by greed. We separate ourselves from on another. This is not the spiritual path of the Creator.

Un-connect yourself from the influence of the television, and reconnect yourself with the Earth. In the words of Hopi elder, Floyd Red Crow Westerman, "If you're not spiritually connected to the Earth and understand the spiritual reality of how to live on Earth, it's likely you will not make it."

You can learn a lot from an Indian. Did you know, the

Constitution of the United States is based on the Iroquois Confederacy? On October 1, 1988, the United States Congress passed a resolution that recognizes the influence the Iroquois had upon establishing the foundation of our freedom. The first people of this land didn't use money. They took care of each other and traded skills, furs, whatever. Food was usually shared by the entire tribe. No one went hungry, unless everyone was hungry.   Kind of like, "The Collective." The tribe relied on each others abilities, and for the most part, the Indians were happy. That is, until a bunch of pushy Europeans came around and actually forced the entire Indian Nation into a world they did not belong. A world based on consumerism and greed.

The wisdom the indigenous people of the world fight so hard to save is an insight that mankind can not afford to lose anymore than we can afford to lose the words of Jesus, Buddha, or Allah. Put the pieces of the puzzle together and you will see the entire picture and understand.

Jesus said, "Split a piece of wood; I am there. Lift up a stone, and you will find me there," so says the lost Gospel of Thomas 1:77. By the way, a Church is made up of wood and stone. Maybe that's why the Gospel of Thomas was lost? Be your own leader; read and think for yourself.

Walk The Talk

"Let us always meet each other with a smile, for the smile is the beginning of love." - Mother Teresa

How many times have you logged onto your Facebook page, or some other social network, and seen a quote, or watched a video that moves you? Do you live by the words and images that touch your heart? Do you smile and say hello to all the people who cross your path throughout the day? Did you feed the homeless person standing on the corner with a sign asking for help? Or did you judge him or her from high upon your pedestal not worthy of your time and money?

The people of this planet are crying out in hunger; hungry for love. Take for instance the wars in the Middle East. These wars have produced the highest number of soldiers to ever return to the States with Post Traumatic Stress Syndrome (PTSS); more than Vietnam. Why?

Because we (as human beings) know war is wrong. It's a bad thing. Jesus scolded Peter, when Peter had cut off an ear of a servant. Peter thought he was defending Jesus. "Then Jesus said to him, "Put your sword back into its sheath, for all who take the sword will perish by the sword,"" Matthew 26:52. Then Jesus healed the servant's ear.

Jesus condemns killing in the name of God once again, in John 16:2-3, ". . . the hour is coming when everyone who kills you will think he is offering worship to God. They will do this because they have not known either the Father or me."

And at John 14:34-35, Jesus says, "I give you a new commandment: love one another. This is how all will know you are my disciples, if you have love for one another."

If we truly lived by the words of Jesus, as so many people claim, then one would have to have a really hard time justifying killing another human being.

Don't get me wrong. I'm not condemning any soldiers. I admire their courage and conviction. Most soldiers are honorable people. I was once a soldier myself, within ten months of graduating from high school. I was blessed that it was a time of peace when I served. Unlike my uncle who died at age nineteen in Vietnam.

Still, if we truly were living by those ten easy rules that God gave to Moses, and the new commandment given by Jesus, there would be no war. And as I scroll through Facebook and see all these wonderful quotes and inspiring photos of nature, I know that the thought is there, but where is the action. The thought alone is not enough.

Mother Teresa use to instruct her nuns to greet everyone they meet with a smile at the beginning of the day, before they stepped out of the mission. I watched her do this it in a movie years ago. But it wasn't until 2010 that I began to incorporate the thought of her words into my own life. Why so long? Because, it isn't easy to look a stranger in the eye and smile.

Somewhere along the line, I had learned to avoid eye contact. By avoiding eye contact, I didn't have to acknowledge the pain and suffering of others. It also kept me safe, because you can not see the real me, if you can't see into my eyes. If you can see into my eyes, you might see my weakness, my insecurities. Then you might use them against me and hurt me. We cut ourselves off from strangers out of fear. If you expect the worst from someone, then that's all you will ever see out of them.

I live in a well-established (older) residential neighborhood. It doesn't have the best of reputations, and parts of it are a little scary. Still, when I cruise down the street, I smile and wave at everyone. Adults, kids, and even the dreaded rebellious teenager, whether they are black, white, brown or yellow, I smile and say hi to them all.

Celia will often stare aimlessly in the other direction, if she happens to be riding with me. Every once in while she'll make a comment like, "You know those kids are thinking, "Why's that crazy cracker waiving at me for?""

Still, I wave. And eventually, some started waving back. Even the tough looking teenagers who use to simply stare me down, will wave back now. They even know my car and will wave to me, before I wave to them sometimes. I smile real big now, and so do they. The Blessed Mother Teresa was right. A smile will spread love.

So take it step further, don't just post pretty things on Facebook and be done for the day. Walk the talk. Be brave and live by the words you hide behind.

"We know only too well that what we are doing is nothing more than a drop in the ocean. But if the drop were not there, the ocean would be missing something," -- Mother Teresa.

Everything counts, even in small amounts.

CHAPTER THREE - The Beach 2011

BP had begun to bulldoze their way along Pensacola Beach in November 2010. And on January 6, 2011, for the first time, I watched the workers drill into the sand with no evidence of oil. I was so full of hope that day. But it was short lived. BP announced they were done; they weren't going to clean the water. They decided it was best to wait for the oil to roll in with the tides, and clean it as it came, as if it was ever really clean at all. And it wasn't long until all that sand became contaminated once again, spreading throughout the dunes, and across the street that divided the island, towards the Santa Rosa Sound.

On Saturday, March 5, a storm rolled through the Gulf of Mexico causing all kinds of wildlife to wash up dead on the beach. I saw a dead seagull with an eyeball on its wing, and a thin red line that resembled an artery ran from the detached wing to the body. And I found another that was completely laid out flat as a pancake, within ten feet of the first gull I had seen. There were thousands of man-o-wars scattered all up and down the entire island. None of which looked healthy at all in comparison with photos I had taken before the oil spill.

Six days later, on a Friday morning, we went back out on the beach. It was a hot sunny day, and the dead stuff was still lying out on the beach as far as the eye could see. Flies were everywhere drawn to the rank odor of death. The tar balls weren't hard to find either. I thought we were standing in a third world country. The blue had faded out of the man-o-wars, and the brown stains became more prominent.

We drove the road towards Navarre, and the sand appeared to be brown and black with white patches here and there. You didn't even have to get out of your car and look for signs of oil. It was that apparent. And it didn't matter which side of the road you were looking at, sound side or ocean view. So imagine my surprise, when I went out to the beach the next day and saw parking lots filled with spring breakers vacationing.

One group of kids had three holes dug in the sand. One guy was buried, while the other two were digging their way to China. We couldn't even see the second guys head.

I looked at Celia and said, "I bet they think these washed out man-o-wars are used rubbers. I ought to tell them that this bag of tar balls is some good Pensacola hash, and make a little money on the side," as we both giggled like women do.

On March 16, just four days later, WEAR TV ran a story about some spring breakers from Missouri, who complained about brown stuff sticking to them, when they came out of the water. And it wasn't washing off of them easily either. One tourist said she thought it was shark poop. Of course it was tar balls.

I rolled laughing! You have brown gooey oil caked on your back and armpit, and all you can do is joke and crack up about it. I might as well laugh too then.

Surrender to the Wind

Wind is a force that brings about change. It can be seen in the white caps of the waves, or in the destruction of a hurricane that's brought about by the gentle wings of a small butterfly. This just goes to prove, for every action in this world, or maybe I should say, "Lack of," there is a reaction.

Since the oil spill, there had been no major hurricanes or tropical storms to hit the Pensacola area, until the first of September, when Tropical Storm Lee crossed the Gulf of Mexico on its way to Texas. The first day when Lee arrived, I went out to the beach, east of Portofino towers. The surf was rough. All you could see was white caps and foam from the waves pounding full force into the sand. The wind was blowing so hard, that it caked sand onto my windshield and began covering portions of the road. The only sea life I saw laying dead upon the beach were jelly fish mixed with small amounts of green sea weed. Still there were enough jelly fish on the beach that it sparkled when the light hit it just right. And someone had left red rose petals, as they had so many other times, when I visited that area of the island.

Two days later, I went back out on the beach. Except this time, not only did I go East of Portofino Towers, I went to the tourist end of the beach too (Casino Beach). There's a long pier there. And the surfers love to ride the waves in that area. I figured since there was nothing to report on out by Portofino Towers, I might as well shoot some footage of the surfers. All I could find was a couple of brave dudes floating on their boards, and some others looking on from the beach. The water was just way to choppy to catch a wave and do anything with it. Not to mention, the worry of having your own board crack your skull open.

But what I did find on the beach was what looked like brown sheets of stale cake frosting in a large area right beside the pier. There were footprints in it. I scratched my head wondering why anyone would step in what looked like a dog with the diarrhea left behind. And on the opposite side of the pier, there was a line of brown sea foam that matched the black streaks left in the sand. A child played no more than twenty feet away digging at a large hole in the sand. Another child chasing the suspicious looking foam ran up where I was filming, and the camera caught her tiny bare feet standing in the contaminated sand. The beach to me looked horrific! It was like the Gulf of Mexico spewed all over the place.

Within twelve hours of uploading the video to YouTube, Good Morning America sent an e-mail asking my permission to use the video. In part the letter read, "We would like to request permission to show this video on GMA (and across our ABC News shows and platforms, which is seen worldwide an on all media). It's a phenomenal video which would really enhance our news reporting."

I responded by giving them permission to use the video and

added that we here in the South are highly appreciative for the time and consideration.

But no one I know has ever seen the video on Good Morning America or on any other ABC network. I think they were more interested in the storm footage, than they were in showing America, "Hey, the oil is still here! Look at this stink hole you've been swimming in this past summer."

All the same, the video went viral anyway. And again, YouTube extended their Partnership Program to me, but getting paid felt like selling out, so I never opted for the option.

Ten days later, at dusk on September 13, I was out on the beach again to meet Maia and the gang to return the Gulf water that we had all been meditating on, for the past month. After we left the pier, we went to the waters edge to collect new water. The water was gentle, and brown oily foam lied along the top of the water, brushing back and forth along the shore. About then feet away, we collected the water we were to take home. When I brought the water home and had a good look at it, I could see it had a yellow tint to it. And the small amount of sand that collected in my glass jar seemed to stick together forming little yellow balls.

Then on September 15, just two days later, Celia and I went out on the beach, for the sole purpose to relax. It was a beautiful day and the temperature was bearable, in the seventies. Again, we went East of Portofino Towers, out on walk-out number twenty-seven. We sat our chairs out, and Celia walked the beach, while I sat quietly admiring the fatal beauty. We hadn't even been there twenty minutes, when it started to rain. Celia quickly returned to our little habitat on the beach.

"Damn, where did this rain come from?" I asked, totally surprised by it all.

"I don't know? Strange," she replied.

"I left the sun roof open! Can you get the chairs?"

"Yeah, I got them," Celia said, as I scrambled for the truck.

Thank God it wasn't a heavy downpour, but it did get me thinking. Everything happens for a reason. So when Celia made it to the parking lot, I asked her, "Do you want to take a ride, while this rain passes over?"

"Sure. Why not?"

"Let's drive toward Navarre," I suggested.

And before we made it to the first pull off, once we crossed into National Seashores, I knew we were going to take this ride one more time, after we found a place to turn around. Because the sand looked that bad! But once we arrived at the parking lot, where we were able to turn around, I found myself on the sand video taping the same ugly stale looking cake frosting dog doo doo that I had seen on Casino beach during Tropical Storm Lee. It was everywhere. And again, there were footprints tracking through the oil that had been uncovered by the wind.

When we did finally pull out of parking lot, I noticed that right across the street, on the sound side of the road, was a large tide pool surround by dark brown sand. After we did our second drive by with Celia driving and a video camera in my hand, we went Casino Beach for Bloody Marys. Knowing that this part of the beach was a tourist area, I figured it would of been all cleaned up. But I could see brown tide pools from the walkway.

"Come on, let's go down there and take look," I suggested to Celia.

"No, I really don't need to see anymore. It's just too sad."

"Then explain to me why it rained on us, when there were no rain clouds in the sky? If it wasn't for the rain, we would have never seen any of this! We were guided here for a reason. You know this is what we must do."

Half heartedly Celia walked with me down to the shoreline. As I video taped the black, brown and yellow sand along the water, a seagull cried out. He was sitting in one of the tide pools filled with brown water. When he seen me hesitate, he began squawking and looked up to the sky, then back down to the water. He splashed at it with his beak, as if to say, "Hey, come look at this crap!"

So I did. There was some kind of black stringy goo along the edge of this tide pool. And there was thick brown bubbly crap within the water as well (most likely Corexit). There were two soft grey feathers oblivious to the wind that stuck to the goo. And I'm thinking, I know this birds going to die. There are three more gulls sitting on the beach with their legs folded below them. They look sick. And there's people everywhere playing in the tide pools and digging in the sand. And for the first time, since the oil spill, I said something to a young couple who was sitting in the black sand. "Do you know you're sitting in oil?!"

I said it so matter of factly, like how could you miss it idiot! That the dude looked at me firmly like, what? You didn't just say, what I thought you said did you?

Surprised by my own spontaneous outburst, I said nothing more and walked on.

Shout It Loud

When 2011 rolled around, I really didn't have any hope for myself, let alone mankind. But as the end of the year drew near, I could feel little seeds of encouragement growing inside. We had gone from silence and dead birds falling from the skies, to a time when thousands were standing up across America protesting the banks on Wall Street, our corporate government, and the environmental injustices that our nation faced. The movement was called "Occupy."

In Florida, Trisha Springstead and Trisha James had stepped up and made headway regarding the health of Gulf Coast victims of the Deepwater Horizon Disaster. And in Alabama, Michele Walker-Harmon and Kimberly McCuiston had risen as leaders in their communities, by arranging a BP demonstration during the National Shrimp Festival in Gulf Shores, Alabama on Saturday, October 15th. In comparison to the thousands of people who showed up for the festival, only a couple dozen people demonstrated. Some may find this discouraging. But considering this to be the first demonstration that had taken place, east of the Louisiana boarder, since capping the Macondo well, I applauded the day.

In contrast to Hands Across the Sand, these two women had to get a permit to demonstrate. At first the city refused their request. Then after the City had spoken to the ladies attorneys there was a reversal by city officials, with restrictions. The demonstration had to be two hundred feet away from the festival, and on the beach.

And the use of a bull horn or any other type of devise, electric or battery operated, was prohibited. And my favorite was, if you were wearing a t-shirt that was associated with the oil spill, you were not allowed to walk through the festival to get to the beach; you had to walk the beach to get to the demonstration. In turn, this meant one would have no access to a toilet, or food and water, without walking a mile in sand to a restaurant. Considering the protest began at noon and was to end at 4 p.m., it made for a long day in the sun. But I can say that I did walk into the festival area to use the bathroom and get a drink on two occasions, without any hassle. And we didn't disperse until 4:30, without dispute from the police or security. I guess they didn't see our small group as a threat.

But what they didn't realize at the time is that our little demonstration was photographed and video taped and plugged in to the masses across the Internet, before the day was over. And within twenty-four hours those twenty-four people shared their day with all their friends, who in turn shared the event with their friends. As a result, our story touched the lives of thousands. And that day will continue to live on, and inspire others as well.

When I first arrived at the demonstration, a young man came up to us and told us of how he believed the local television stations, when they said it was safe to swim in the water, at the end of May, in 2010. As a result, he took his three year old son swimming in the Gulf of Mexico. The child had an existing blood disorder, where his blood would not clot. After being exposed to the toxic water, the child had to get blood transfusions three times a week, in contrast to three times a year, which was the procedure before the child swam in the in the toxic waters of the Gulf.

One person, claiming to be a Gulf Coast resident, left a comment on the video page criticizing the father for taking his child into the water in the first place, and then followed up with, "There wasn't even any heavy oil on the beach, until June."

Personally, I know for a fact that on May 31, 2010, Memorial Day, the last day Celia and I swam in the Gulf, you couldn't taste the salt in the water. It wasn't until months later we discovered that Corexit needs salt in order to work properly. In other words, we were swimming in toxic water as early as the Memorial Day weekend.

And at the protest, Kimberly McCuiston showed us several scars and lesions upon her legs from October 2010. She said, "These things will itch. And then they'll break open, and bleed. And it's an endless cycle. That's what they do. And I'm detoxing, but they don't go away."

Trisha Springfield of Brooksville, Florida was the first to speak at the demonstration. Trisha is a Registered Nurse, who holds a Masters in Biological Science, and she is the President and patented inventor of organic skin products. She had been fighting the Center for Disease Control, and the Food and Drug Administration all the way up to the White House, for years, as a proponent for Morgellons Disease.

Because we didn't have the advantage of electronic equipment, Trisha would speak a sentence or two, and the rest of us would repeat her words, as we faced the crowd of tourist along the boardwalk.

"This is what we did," Trisha began.

And on cue, the crowd repeated loudly, "This is what we did!"

"Trisha James went to the EPA and FDA web site." The protesters repeated her words again.

"They baffled you with bullshit!" The crowd gladly conveyed her words once again, with emphasis on the word, "Bullshit."

Trisha loudly declared, "They blinded you with science!"

As the protesters channeled her message across the barren sand that separated them from the crowd, Trisha spoke boldly, "You can have one shrimp. Or thirteen grams. One day. Over five years. For an eighty kilogram. Human being. In order to not to get cancer!"

"You can have. Twelve grams of oysters. That is three quarters of an oyster. In one day. Over five years. In order to not to get cancer!"

"You can have forty nine grams of fin fish! That's fish with fins (emphasis on fins) in one day. For an eighty kilogram human being over five years in order not to get cancer!"

As Trisha spoke, her hand would fly in the air as loudly as her words, "That includes Lymphoma! Leukemia! Blood born cancers! That includes bone marrow cancer! Stomach cancer! Pancreatic cancer! Kidney cancer!. Liver cancer!. And brain cancer!"

Everyone applauded loudly; finally feeling justified as to why we were there that day. Captain Lori Deangelis, of Dolphin Queen Cruises, from Orange Beach, Alabama was the second speaker at the demonstration and had this to say, "Five hundred and sixty two dead dolphins since the BP oil catastrophe."

Again the band of protesters repeated her words loudly, directing their attention to the festival goers on the boardwalk.

"Experts say as many as fifty times more dolphin deaths could be happening for every one that is found." The protesters dwelled on.

"Dolphin deaths are ten times the normal amount yearly. Dolphin health equals human health."

Again the crowd of protesters began to clap loudly, after they repeated Lori's declaration to the dolphins.

Captain Paul Grogan spoke next. Paul was at ground zero of the Deepwater Horizon explosion and was one of the Captains who was told to stop spraying water onto the fire.

"There's ten boats working with NOAA (National Oceanic and Atmospheric Administration)." Paul seemed a little uncomfortable, but continued, "And they're out there finding oil everyday." The protesters cloned his every word.

"They caught over a hundred and fifty sharks and cut them open. They got oil inside them. So we got to save the sharks. We got to save the dolphins. And we got to save us," as Paul shrugged his shoulders with a speed boat roaring behind him, "and we got to save the Gulf!"

The protesters cheered loudly, as the boisterous noisy boat disappeared, and spectators began to stop in front of the tent to hear more.

Cherri Foytlin was the last to speak. She began by introducing Michele Walker-Harmon and Kimberly McCuiston, of Gulf Shores, Alabama. "They fought hard to be here today."

The crowd repeated Cherri's words. "And they want to tell the truth. Because they love you."

As we hammered her words, a new sense of strength filled me up.

"Because they're protecting you. They want you to have good safe jobs. They want your children to grow up happy and healthy. They want your water to be clean. Because they love you."

I had to smile whenever we repeated, "Because we love you." Because we really do. We weren't there to hate, or cause business owners to lose money, we were there because it breaks our hearts to see children playing in poison, and misguided tourist eating seafood from the Gulf of Mexico.

"We came here today. From all the states on the Gulf Coast. Because we love you," Cherri continued. ". . . And we don't care if you think we're silly. And we don't care if you think we're lying. Because if you think the government is telling you the truth. Ask the people affected by Agent Orange. Ask the nine eleven first responders. Ask the people of Michigan oil spill. Ask the people of Yellowstone oil spill. Ask the people of Exxon Valdez oil spill."

"Because we love you. We stand here. Because the oil's still here. So are we. And we will not go away. Because we love you. God bless the Gulf."

Amen.

CHAPTER FOUR – The Year 2012

The year 2012 began with an attack by Congress to open the Eastern Gulf (Florida) to offshore drilling. H.R. 3410 also known as the Energy Security and Transportation Jobs Act allowed for oil exploration off of the shores of Florida.

WEAR TV (ABC) interviewed a couple of locals regarding the subject. Maggie Halsey, owner of Barefoot Weddings, in Okaloosa County had this to say, "I can not believe, after everything that we've just gone through with the oil spill that they would pass something like this. Ah, that I mean that's absurd!"

The other concern seemed to be based on the military stations here in the Panhandle. Jim Breitenfeld, with the Defense Support Initiative said, "There is no positive impact that relates to the military presence in Northwest Florida. The Eglin ranges help bases all over the state hang onto military missions. All this does is put a big black checkmark at the top of the list of things that make these bases vulnerable."

The news reporter, Laura Hussey wrapped the story up with, "At this point there's only a small chance of it passing."

And that was the last I heard regarding H.R. 3410, or drilling in the Eastern Gulf, until the following year.

February 17, 2012 started as a promising day. Celia and I decided to visit the Gulf, and we actually saw three or four dolphins swimming near the shore. But after a hike in the dunes, we found little clear crystal silicone things with brown and black stains on them. They were soft like jelly.

One person suggested that it could of been polyacrylate superabsorbent gels derived from petroleum, often used in women's sanitary napkins. And apparently used on the dunes due to the fact that polyacrylate holds moisture. But it was never tested. And common sense seemed to dictate, why would you use an unnatural product on something that grows in that area naturally anyway? So, we really don't know what it was.

But what was even more interesting was that the dunes were no longer there. The fence was all broken along the beach, and it appeared that someone was either using the area to bury wildlife, or they were using the dune sand to cover the sand on the beach itself, which was stained black in some places along the shoreline.

Celia and I had found a turtle skull in that area just three months previous. And we had found a dead pelican buried in those dunes just a couple weeks later, in March. We also found a giant mound of sand that a bulldozer had pushed aside. The tire tracks were still etched in the sand two to three feet wide. There were also human (shoe) tracks leading back to that mound of sand.

That same day in March, we found the wide tire tracks on Navarre Beach too. There was a fluffy brown substance mixed in the sand in that same area where the tire tracks were. It was piled thick. I asked around, but no one could tell me what it was. One thing for sure though, it was not a natural part of the landscape.

Then on February 23, the Pensacola New Journal (PNJ) posted a swimming ban at Bayou Texar, at Bayview Park, ". . . due to the potential for high bacterial levels." The article went on to say, ". . . the level of bacteria has exceeded the level established by the state guidelines."

Meaning, yes indeed the water wasn't safe to swim in. To say there was a "potential" was a misuse of the word.

While PNJ was publishing articles such as this anywhere, but on the front page, BP was still cramming their television commercials through every T.V. set as possible in America. It was more than evident that the ads were working. Spring break brought 5,000 more vehicles through the toll booth on the beach than in 2011; 10,000 more in comparison to 2010.

On March 29, PNJ posted another story in the middle of the paper that stated tar balls were more than a nuisance. The study was conducted by an Auburn microbiologist named Cova Arias. Her specialty is oysters, not tar balls. But since her lab is located on Dauphin Island, when the tar balls began to wash up, the professor and her team decided test a few.

They discovered that the tar balls were full of bacteria, including Vibrio vulnificus, also known as the flesh eating bacteria. It is the leading cause of death from eating bad oysters. V vulnificus can travel through cuts in the skin, and puts people with suppressed immune systems or chronic health conditions, such as diabetes, at high risk.

The Associated Press wrote, "In fact, they discovered that the tar balls had up to 100 times more of that particular bacteria than the water they floated in and 10 times more than the sand they rested on."

Other information soon became available as well, regardless of litigation. On April 10, WKRG (CBS), channel 5, out of Mobile, Alabama reported, "If the Gulf were a patient in the hospital, it would be in the critical care unit," citing a study by the National Wildlife Federation.

On April 15, the Tampa Bay Times ran a story in which an independent geologist, Rip Kirby, discovered by accident that dispersant mixed with oil soaks into the skin when wet. His assistant, a grad student was helping collect samples in the water one day. Kirby was showing his student how a tar ball will glow orange under an ultra violet light, when he turned the light onto the student's legs, they were still speckled orange. And a shower did not wash it away. It was still glowing in the skin.

On April 17, Al Jazeera News released a YouTube video regarding a subject that no national media in the United States would touch -

eyeless shrimp. They had a biologist named Dr. Felder, who showed the oil that the shrimp had ingested, as he explained the consequences of reproduction within the shrimp population. As well as the effects the contamination will have on the food chain.

Al Jazeera even went as far to ask government agencies for a comment. But none them would even acknowledge that a problem with the Gulf seafood existed. The Food & Drug Administration (FDA), and the Environmental Protection Agency (EPA) referred AlJazeera to the National Oceanic & Atmosphere Administration (NOAA). But NOAA refused to comment due to the impending lawsuit against BP.

The Al Jazeera story just added fuel to the fire of the injustices our own government was committing towards the very people they were suppose to represent.

In addition, Dolphins continued washing up on the northern Gulf shores at increasing rates, suffering from liver and lung disease.

Then, on the 2nd Anniversary of the Deepwater Horizon Disaster, April 20th, WEAR TV actually did a story on the sick fish in the Gulf. They interviewed a charter boat captain who stated, "Word like that getting around is just not good at all for anybody." -- Cha-Ching!

It just hit me like a ton of bricks. When are people going to realize that putting up this front is not benefiting the community? Not to mention putting the lives of other human beings at stake for a dollar. This egotistical attitude is nothing short of being criminal. And it encompasses a large population. I don't think I have ever really realized how "Me" oriented people can be, until I saw this man speak. He's probably one of the boaters who ran over the oil booms that were put in place to protect the bay, back in 2010. Because he couldn't deal with a 10 p.m. curfew! Me! Me! Me!

The Deepwater Horizon Disaster was downplayed from the word go. It was like watching the first Jaws movie, where the mayor is running around denying the shark attacks, regardless of the evidence that swimming in the water is detrimental to your health.

This was the Mayor of Orange Beach, Alabama, Tony Kennon's, reaction to the Deepwater Horizon Disaster, on June 17, 2010. One week before heavy crude hit Pensacola Beach, which is located approximately 20 miles East of Orange Beach, the Mayor participated in an online discussion regarding President Obama's speech on the gulf oil spill clean up, with the Washington Post. The Mayor is introduced, and the Washington Post asked one question, then a person labeled "Tourism" jumps in the discussion:

Tourism: Hi, thanks for taking questions and comments. I just want to note that I was in the Gulf region this past weekend, and everything was fine. The seafood was tasty (and came from the gulf), the sites looked good, the only problem was that it was hot! I hope people start to realize that there's still a ton of safe places to go and things to do on the coast.

Tony Kennon: I think that's exactly right. We've only had one week since the incident where we actually had oil on our beaches and that was this past week. So the perception that our beaches are totally shut down is false. But there are going to be times when oil will be in the water, on the beach and can be a problem. But it's intermittent in nature.

The Deepwater Horizon well wasn't capped until July 15, 2010, approximately one month after this conversation. Just sitting on the beach was putting your health at risk, at that time. People who work in oil refineries wear masks for a reason. The crude oil vapors alone are toxic to the human body.

On the weekend of May 5th, 2012 an underwater tar mat was discovered in Perdido Pass, while crews were digging sand out of the channel. Suddenly denial turned into, "We were not surprised by the discovery," said the Orange Beach mayor, "I begged BP to take care of the oil countless times," as reported by WEAR TV, on May 9.

Only two days later, on May 11, television stations across the area were broadcasting that the test showed the oil in Perdido Pass wasn't BP's. Imagine that. When you declare that your beach is free of oil and it doesn't exist anymore, then you just give BP a free pass to deny all responsibility. Remember, this is 2012. Two years after the 2010 interview with The Washington Post.

Of course the facts didn't add up, and we all know it belonged to BP. Mayor Kennon told Fox 10 News, "There was oil sheen coming from essentially nowhere. The Coast Guard had investigated earlier could not find a source from a fuel dock, or a vessel, and there was a putrid smell that we know very well comes from a tar mat, when it's broken open. You don't have that smell with a normal fuel spill, whether it be from a vessel or not."

Orange Beach had to pay for their own test, which cost in the neighborhood of $2,000, which is why you don't see a whole lot of independent tests, I suppose.

Then on June 4, 2012, dead fish were reported to be washing up on Gulf Shores, Alabama, by WPMI out of Mobile. It was the third fish kill in the past week in Baldwin County. It was blamed on warm water (in June). This explanation was even attributed to the dead fish that floated on the water in Mobile Bay, around Fairhope, the previous week before.

I even read one article where one family spent the weekend fishing off of Gulf State Pier (Alabama), who spotted several dead fish floating upon the water and washing up on the shore, with a white foam surrounding them.

By June 23rd, the white foam had found its way into Escambia Bay. I stood on Scenic Highway, looking out over Interstate 10, from Pensacola, in total disbelief. White fluffy foam was streaked across the water for as far as my eye could see. And as I drove along the water, I could even catch glances of the foam in between the houses that sat along the waters edge, as I drove north towards Highway 90.

I didn't know it at the time, but apparently reports of a white foam being sprayed on the Gulf of Mexico began on June 13th, from fishermen off the coast of Venice, Louisiana. The Coast Guard told Plaquemines Parish officials that it was a mock dispersant, being sprayed by a company out of Mississippi. Yet the fishermen complained that it caused itching and burning.

On June 25th, just two days after discovering the white foam in Escambia Bay, there was a large fish kill in Bonita Bay, off Lillian Hwy. Flounder, Red Snapper, and Croaker were found. This time the news media left the viewer believing that it was a storm that was most likely the culprit. In all of these fish kills, we were told that test would be performed, but the results have never been made public.

In an interview dated July 3rd, Plaquemines Parish President, showed photos of the white foam, and was asking environmental officials and the coast guard for answers. He went onto to say that originally they were told that the foam in the pictures was mosquito spray. Then they were told that they were spraying water as a test for dispersants. But as the Plaquemines Parish President explained (common sense) there was something more than water being sprayed, in quantities not seen since the Deepwater Horizon Disaster. "We just can't get any answers," he said.

June just seemed to be a bad month. It's hard enough to fight our own government to get some answers, let alone fight with the people with whom you share a common cause.

Divided We Fall

About mid June, an Alabama Gulf Coast leader began driving to Navarre Beach to go swimming. Celia and I hadn't been in the Gulf since Memorial Day 2010. And I had no issues with any person playing in the Gulf water. I believe in choice. But then the Alabama activist, who's name I rather not mention, went on Facebook and told everyone that it was safe to swim in that area.

Now remember, Navarre Beach is located on the same island as Pensacola Beach; Navarre sits just East of the National Seashores that divides Santa Rosa County, from Escambia County. Which left me feeling somewhat insulted. "How dare she come over to my sand box and tell everyone that everything is just peachy over here."

Needless to say, I sent her a personal message through Facebook asking her to quit telling people it was safe to swim in this area, but she refused. And then she brought the disagreement out in public. What followed was a division between activists.

As a result of our disagreement, on June 21st, I took my camera to the western side of Navarre Beach (The National Seashores) and shot some video of streaked black sand along the shoreline. Still, the Alabama girls argued that what we were seeing was not oil and that this black sand was normal.

So I shot another video of some sand that I had taken from the beach on that same day. I had allowed that sand to dry for 2 days, on a paper plate, in my air conditioned home. Then I compared with sand that I had taken from the dune area a couple of months before, that had been stored in a jar the entire time.

You could visibly see that there was a difference in the texture, and the color. The sand from the shoreline was chunky and thick. It stuck together. The sand from the dunes was soft, white, and light as a feather. I used purple colored paper to show everyone the difference in the two samples. I picked it up and rubbed it between my fingers to show people how the shoreline sand globed together.

It may not have been science, but I think with a little common sense, one would most certainly draw the conclusion that something was making that black sand stick together. Like, maybe oil?

Shortly after the sand test, a friend of mine stopped by and saw the jar of sand sitting on the coffee table. I turned my back to get something and by the time I turned back around, she had popped the lid off of the jar and stuck her nose to it. The look on her face had me rolling on the floor laughing. I asked her, "How did it smell?"

"It smells like death. Like something died up in that jar." And she isn't an activist by any means, and was totally clueless as to what was in the jar. She only saw sand.

All the same, I pushed a little further and posted a request on group pages asking people to send me photos of black sand along the seashore, before the 2010 disaster. No one was able to produce any pictures. And to this day, they still haven't. Even the most vivid skeptic has yet to show me a photo. Still, I spent hours going through our own personal photos of the beach, video included, but I found nothing showing me the black shorelines that I see today.

But, all of my posting and videos made their way to a friend of a man, from Louisiana, who had been swimming on Navarre Beach (the nude beach), in June. His name was Dave. He said he was only in the water for a minute, and could tell instantly that something was wrong. So he left the water immediately. His skin was burning and he felt week. He couldn't drive back to New Orleans's because he felt so bad. So he pulled over at a rest stop between Alabama and Mississippi and spent the night. Two days later his skin started peeling massively. A week later he was covered with strange black moles surrounded by clear circles.

Then another story surfaced. They may possibly be related. This story came from YouTube user, Nolabutterfly. "Within a couple of hours of helping a friend put lotion on his feet, after he got really sick from swimming in the Gulf, I started itching and burning. Though I washed my hands . . . it must of clung to my hands, and when I went to the bathroom later, and . . . well, you get the picture . . . needless to say, the next day my boyfriend had a burn where he/we NEVER got a burn before. It literally got scabbed!"

Then in August, Surfrider Foundation released their Current Concerns of the Beach Report. The report stated, "The concentration of oil PAH's in the samples collected during 2011 remained as high (and hence as toxic) as samples found in early days of the disaster."

Furthermore they stated, "Greater concentrations of the oil are found in the plunge step area of the beach. This area is generally within a few feet of the waterline and is where children most commonly play."

This supported my assertion that the "black" sand along the shoreline is most likely contaminated as well. It was explained that the plunge step area, works like a street curb. Everything accumulates there.

August 4, 2012 was the Hands Across the Sand protest. It had become a world wide event. In Pensacola there were about two hundred participants, while Gulf Shores, Alabama only had four participants.

By August 11th, seeing support slipping away, the Alabama activists agreed it was time to come together once again and to set aside our differences for the common cause.

And so began my lessons in compassion. There is no room for ego in this battle for clean water and clean air. It is going to take a majority of the human population worldwide to rid ourselves of the toxins we have spilled all over the Earth and in the atmosphere.

You're not always going to like everybody, so instead of focusing on the differences, focus on the common goals. Don't divide yourself from others, unite instead! We are so much more powerful together. When you hear your ego talking, look to your heart and remember who you are. The person standing across from you is an aspect of yourself.

Still, there will be storms. And on August 28th, Isaac passed through the Gulf as a tropical storm, eventually hitting Louisiana as a hurricane. Pensacola beach was trashed. The Gulf of Mexico had spewed black sand and thick sheets of goo everywhere. At the pier there were large amounts of what appeared to be sea grass lying on the beach.

I found a video from where Tropical Storm Arlene had hit us directly, back in 2005. When you compare video from today to the 2005 footage, you can clearly see that the black sand and goo were not an issue seven years back. In addition, you can clearly see that the sea foam from 2005 isn't brown either.

On September 4th, local geologists were still finding tar balls on Walton Beaches (approximately 36 miles East of Pensacola Beach). WJHG (NBC) out of Panama City interviewed Rip Kirby - "The advertising campaign that BP has successfully placed, which has generated a lot of business on the coast was perhaps overly optimistic. And that uh, signage that advises about the health risk with contact of tar product on the beach is missing and should be out here."

On November 15th, the Justice Department announced that it had reached an agreement BP to resolve all criminal claims against BP, by the United States government. BP pleaded guilty to eleven felony accounts related to the deaths of the eleven men who died, due to neglect.

BP also pleaded guilty to the violations of the Clean Water Act, and the Migratory Bird Treaty Act. And finally, BP pleaded guilty to obstruction of Congress for lying about the amount of the oil that was flowing out of the well.

BP was to pay four billion dollars in criminal penalties. But there was no sentencing or prison time for any of the C.E.O.'s. Corporations by law are to be recognized as persons, yet no one ever does the time for the crime. A clear example as to why we need to amend the U.S. Constitution to clarify the definition of a "person."

2010 wasn't only the year of the biggest environmental spill that the United States had ever seen; it was also the year that the U.S.

Supreme Court gave corporations the right to be considered persons, via *"Citizens United v Federal Election Commission."*

The Court ruled that limits on campaign/political donations from corporations infringed on the corporations First Amendment right. The argument being that the U.S. Constitution was created to protect "individual" rights. The important word here being "Person." **Therefore, it does not apply to a corporation of many.**

Not to mention, Citizens opened the door for more money to flow into the political arena. And never has it been as apparent as it is today. Politicians no longer work for the people, they work for the corporations. Every time Congress can't pass a budget, it's not your and my interest they have at heart; it is their corporate sponsors they are fighting so hard for.

Come December 9th, I found my video camera in my hand again. At walk-out #27, the beach was eroding away. The wooden walkway itself was closed due to the huge drop off at the end, where it met the beach. Again, we found thick patches of black sand along the shoreline. And this time, we found what appeared to be Corexit floating in the Gulf at the shore as well; a bubbly, thick, brown foam.

As December 21st approached, the last date of the Mayan calendar (known as Doomsday to some), I prepared and waited anxiously for a new spiritual high. And what an awakening that was!

CHAPTER FIVE – The Year 2013

"I feel like if you are giving reasons as to why someone else's fight to be heard for justice doesn't matter to you. You must understand that you are explaining the exact same reasons your battle doesn't matter to them. We have to start mattering to each other, if we want to win" - Cherri Foytlin

Idle No More

For those of you who say the Mayan's were wrong about December 2012; I dare to challenge your opinions. There was a shift in awareness among humanity. And "Idle No More" was proof of that.

Idle No More is an indigenous movement born in Canada that was started by four young women, Nina WIlson, Sheelah McLean, Syliva McAdam, and Jessica Gordon, in early October 2012. It began with a piece of Canadian legislation known as Bill C-45 (also known as the Jobs and Growth Act), which removed over ninety percent of the environmental policies that protected the water and land. Thousands of rivers and lakes are now unprotected and open to the oil and gas industries to do as they wish, mostly on reservations, while eliminating treaty rights.

- On December 9, 2012, Chief Theresa Spence of the Attawapiskat people drew attention to the Idle No More movement when she went on a hunger strike after Prime Minister Stephen Harper refused to speak to her. She actually camped out on an island on the Ottawa River, across from Parliament Hill with the hope of convincing the Canadian government to take First Nations concerns seriously.

Then on December 21st, came the flash mobs of drummers and round dances. YouTube videos flooded the Internet. The excitement of such a gathering ran through me like this was the day I've been waiting for my entire life. I could feel the power of the drums flow from my feet and straight into my heart. A new day had began, unity in the defense of our Earth Mother.

On January 11, 2013, Idle No More called for a "Global Day of Action," and I was more than happy to oblige. A handful of us protested in downtown Pensacola from 11:00 am to 1:00 pm; targeting the lunch time crowd. There were less than ten of us, but we did make the evening news locally, as well as the local newspaper.

Cherri Foytlin contacted me right after Idle No More announced the Global Day of Action, and asked if I would be interested in joining her with an Idle No More Gulf Coast chapter.

Cherri followed up by hosting an I.N.M.G.C. protest in New Orleans, on January 20th. At least eighty people participated in the event, including Poarch Creek, the United Houma Nation, the Isle de Jean Charles Band of Biloxi-Chitimacha-Choctaw, and the Grand Caillou/Dulac Band of Biloxi-Chitimacha-Choctaw. Four young people from the Texas Tar Sands Blockade were present as well.

The Tar Sands Blockade was a result of the Keystone Pipeline, which was intended to transport oiled sand (often referred to as tar sands or bitumen) from Alberta, Canada to the Gulf Coast refineries, where it would be eventually shipped to China for consumption.

Tar Sands, found mainly in Canada, is a sticky hydrocarbon that is so thick that it has to be diluted with lighter hydrocarbons or heated in order for it to flow through a pipeline. Because of the sandy texture, it can destroy a pipeline in a short amount of time. There is no question of "if" it will leak, but rather "when" will it leak?

Methods of extracting tar sands include water flooding, gas injection, and strip mining. Needless to say, once they have worked an area over, the land is left dead and barren. Furthermore, it is very expensive to process and among the dirtiest forms of fossil fuel there is.

The number of jobs that the pipeline would create in the United States once it is completed is thirty to forty new American jobs. And the price American's will pay for that pipeline? Just ask the people of Kalamazoo, Michigan, who are still reeling from the Enbridge pipeline that broke in 2010, just days after the Deepwater Horizon Disaster.

To stand with our sisters and brothers to the North, in Canada, only made our cause stronger here along the Gulf Coast. Environmental groups grew and expanded. Especially after land owners in Texas and Oklahoma lost parcels to TransCanada, who claimed imminent domain. TransCanada, a Canadian company, is the operator of the proposed Keystone XL Pipeline. How does a foreign corporation have a right to claim imminent domain?

Before Cherri introduced the Texas Tar Sands Blockade, at the I.N.M.G.C. demonstration, she gave a short speach regarding the Keystone pipeline.

"It's destroying the Earth up North. The tar sands, it's a scar on Mother Earth. And it brings nothing but misery. So we went up to D.C., and we were arrested, some of us. And we protested to stop that. Then President Obama came out, and he said they were going to stop the pipeline up North, so they could do an environmental impact, but gave full power to bring it down here in the South. To me it's just another example of how that we are the energy sacrifice zone for the nation. And unfortunately he did not get a lot of resistance from that, from the people who were fighting originally. I'm not saying they don't care, I'm just saying if they have any hopes of fighting that, they better come down and stand with us. That's all I'm saying. Because if that thing goes down through here easily, like a knife through butter, it'll go through up there, I promise. I promise you that."

Four days later, Chief Spence, after six weeks of no solid food, and the others who had joined her, announced on January 24th that they were ending their hunger strike. Chief Spence had to be hospitalized for a short time afterwards.

Four days later, on January 28th, we held our second I.N.M.G.C. demonstration in Pensacola, after a Global Day of Action was called again. We stood in downtown Pensacola during lunch hour with signs in our hands: "No Planet, No Party," "No Drill, No Spill," No War for Oil, "Idle No More 2013." Four new people joined us that day; plus one really cute puppy. But our protest was small in comparison to the New Orleans demonstration just eight days previous. Still, the global days of action were always called on week days, when people had to work, whereas the New Orleans event was a weekend thing.

I was happy, because I felt like I was doing something. No matter how insignificant others made it out to be, it felt good to stand! I spent most of the winter networking and making new friends.

I even spent my 50th birthday with group of friends and activists who were brought together by Dr. Riki Ott. Riki was linking people around the nation to add an amendment to the U.S. Constitution that would designate citizens as "people," removing the power that the corporations were granted by the U.S. Supreme Court's 2010 decision, Citizens United. Riki was determined to stop the use of Corexit in U.S. waters too. She started an online petition to get the EPA to address the issue of removal of Corexit from the approved list of dispersants that can be used on an oil spill, here in the United States. www.ipetitions.com/petition/ban-toxic-dispersants/

She also taught us how to network within our own communities, and how to propose legislation that would hold our local governments accountable in the event of another oil spill.

Joking, we referred to ourselves as "terra cells."

A pleasant birthday surprise came in the form of a news story that same day. On February 7th, WPMI, NBC 15, broke a story about how a federal mandate was responsible for all these red snapper fish needlessly killed while blowing up old oil rigs in the Gulf of Mexico.

"Undercover video obtained by Local 15 shows thousands of pounds of dead fish, mostly red snapper, floating to the surface after one of the controversial demolitions in the Gulf."

"'Good Lord,' marine scientist Dr. Bob Shipp said, when Local 15 showed him the video. "As a scientist, I think it's abominable.'"

The article went on to say that this happens up to three times a week in the Gulf of Mexico. And boy, did people get mad over that. Especially charter boat captains, anglers, and divers, as well the environmentalists.

These old rigs are a danger to ships, yet they have become habitats for many sea creatures and fish. I refer to this news as a pleasant surprise, because it was just another reason to join voices and outlaw deep sea drilling all together.

On February 9th, I met a young lady named Marsha Fuqua, who was organizing a petition drive to save Blackwater State Park (FL) from oil exploration. The state park is located in Santa Rosa County, just one county over from Escambia. I stood with Marsha and the gang one Saturday afternoon and was amazed at how many cars pulled over to sign the petition. In the end, they were successful at stopping the bill that would allow the oil companies to drill within the park. The bill was withdrawn on February 21st.

Meanwhile, on Feb 11th, Pope Benedict XVI announced his resignation. Benedict cited, "Lack of strength of mind and body," when he made his announcement. He was the first pope to resign under his own initiative, since Pope Celestine V, in 1294.

Celestine resigned only after five months as pope, because he wanted to return to his humble life. His successor, Pope Boniface VIII, imprisoned Celestine until his death in 1296, because it was believed that there can only be one pope at a time.

So Benedict's announcement was a big deal. And another indication of the spiritual changes that were unfolding and taking shape. Within thirty days, a new pope would be announced.

In the meantime, on February 25th, the States of Louisiana and Alabama began their litigation against BP, in Federal Court. At first rumors lingered that BP was negotiating a settlement. But Cherri Foytlin had already began a "Full Trial - Full Disclosure" campaign. Without a full trial, the evidence of the effects of the oil spill collected thus far would have been lost to the public.

The day BP went to Court, we had our monthly Gulf Blessing afterwards. We all decided to go to have dinner at, Thai 54, on Pensacola Bay, in Gulf Breeze; right by the three mile bridge. As I was waiting for the others to pay their checks, I stepped outside and noticed a thick whitish substance floating on the water beside the boat docks. It was black as night, but you couldn't miss it.

When morning arrived, I decided to visit the spot again. I was blown away by how much of this stuff was stuck to and floating along the shoreline. It was thick, beige, orange and brown. I dipped a stick in it and the foam stuck to the stick, and it wouldn't shake off. It was stuck to the rocks that lined the shore as well. I crossed the road, to a small park on the other side of the bridge, and there I seen a stream of foam floating across the bay. Some of which had already began to collect right at the shore.

I grabbed a sample of the strange foam, but couldn't find anyone who wanted to test it. Apparently, it cost two thousand dollars or more.

But I did take my sample to my County Commissioner, Gene Valentino. The commissioner had a monthly breakfast meeting, in which he invited his constituents for an informal bitch session. Perfect for presenting something that no one wanted to have anything to do with. I presented the commissioner with a DVD video recording.

At first the commissioner explained that he had the same thing in his yard, and he was told that it was natural. But after I persisted that it was not natural and resembled Corexit, he said it was plant life that lives on the bottom of the floor that eats oil, then it dies. I asked him to have it tested, but his reply was a smack in the face!

He said, in 2010, during the oil spill that they had sent water samples to the State of Florida, and were never given any answer as to what the water tested for. He said he could send it, but don't expect an answer back.

So I kept the sample in the freezer for about a month afterwards, with the hope that word would get around and someone would want it. I ended up throwing it out.

Funny, photos of Dauphin Island, Alabama were showing the very same foam that we were seeing Pensacola Bay, on the same day, February 27th.

And if there ever was a reason to believe that what we were seeing was Corexit or a variation of it, it would be because of incidents like what happened on March 12th. Bayou Perot, 30 miles south of New Orleans, a barge on tug hits a pipeline. The heat was so intense from the fire that all that could be done was to wait for it to burn itself out. The pipeline was believed to be transporting liquefied petroleum gas. The barge was carrying 2,215 barrels of crude oil.

The next day it was announced that Cardinal Jorge Mario Bergoglio, would be named Pope Francis, in honor of St. Francis of Assisi. He was the first from the America's, to be named pope. Francis was designated the environmental pope from the word go. Eventually there was even a new Facebook community page created, called the Catholic Climate Covenant.

Quotes by Pope Francis include:

"Love all creation, for it is harmony."

"So I would like us all to make a serious commitment to respect and protect creation."

"Are we truly cultivating and caring for creation? Or are we exploiting and neglecting it?"

There's even a Franciscan Earth Corps now, inspired by Pope Francis. Their aim is to "transform the world in the spirit of St. Francis of Assisi."

And if you don't know who St. Francis of Assisi (1181-1226) is, he is the Patron Saint of Animals; he also wrote a poem called, "Canticle of the Sun."   In part it goes like this:

"We praise you Lord for all of your creatures, especially for Brother Sun, who is the day through whom you give us light. And he is beautiful and radiant with great spender, of you most high, he bares your likeness.

We praise you Lord for Sister Moon and the stars, in the heavens you have made them bright, precious and fair.

We praise you Lord for Brothers Wind and Air, fair and stormy, all weathers moods, by which you cherish all that you have made.

We praise you Lord for Sister Water, so useful, humble, precious and pure.

We praise you Lord for Brother Fire, through whom you light the night. He is beautiful, playful, robust and strong.

We praise you Lord for Sister Earth who sustains us with her fruits, colored flowers, and herbs."

Sounds kind of Native American, don't you think? There are some who suspect that the Church is taking advantage of the environmental issues that challenge us today, by marketing a climate concerned pope. But then again, it is also an indication of how concerning climate change is on a world wide scale.

Furthermore, considering this poem was written way before the Europeans came to conquer the America's, validates a natural spiritual connection all humans have with the Earth Mother. It is not just an Indigenous thing.

Idle No More called for a three day action right about the same time the new Pope was announced. Again, we joined our brothers and sisters to the North and held a three day event beginning on the twenty-first of March. Day one (Thursday), there were only three of us. We tried to get passer-bys to stop and sign a petition that would put an amendment to the Florida State Constitution on the ballot in 2014 that would keep protected land and waterways from being sold (to God only knows who).

Stopping traffic didn't work as well for us in downtown Pensacola, like it did for Marsha Fuqua, in Milton (Blackwater State Park).

The second day (Friday), people from all over the Gulf showed up. The goal that day was to pass out a flyer that had information regarding Corexit, as well the web address to sign the petition that Riki Ott had started. It didn't work out too well though. It was unusually cold and very windy that day. It made it extremely hard to handle loose paper.

On the third day (Saturday), Steven DuBose, who helped coordinate the event, brought his family and friends, from the Creek Indian tribe. This event was held in the downtown area, at the Farmer's Market. We collected signatures on the Land & Legacy petition and passed out the Corexit Flyer. Steven's family danced and invited us all in a round dance. Afterwards, most of us met at a restaurant and shared in dinner. And that was the last Idle No More event that was held on the in Pensacola, in 2013.

On March 27th, a train derailed in Parker Prairie, Minnesota dumping 952 barrels of tar sands crude. Just two days later, on March 29th, the Exxon tar sands pipeline, known as Pegasus, ruptured in a residential neighborhood in Mayfair, Arkansas. Oil gushed into the city's drainage pond and Lake Conway, the cities water source. The EPA categorized it as a "major spill." Residents were evacuated, but still many reported the same symptoms as we seen here on the Gulf.

What was even more frustrating is that these people had no idea that there was a pipeline running underneath their homes. A local news station, KTHV 11, interviewed one resident who said, "**I had no idea that there was a pipeline out here, I mean, literally right at the corner of the subdivision. Supposed to be a 20-inch pipeline, run from Illinois to Texas. I don't know.**"

So next time you purchase a house, you may want to check the deed and see who owns the mineral rights. This type of deception is the new craze sweeping across the nation. Since fracking has come to the forefront, it's been discovered that the same practice is occurring in Pennsylvania as well as in Florida.

At the time of the Mayfair, Arkansas incident, Obama was pondering the Keystone Pipeline that was widely associated with Canadian tar sands. So it was no big surprise when Exxon quit using the word tar sands and began calling the heavy oil, "Bitumen," which has historically been associated with asphalt.

In the meantime, on April 8th, you could drive along Pensacola Beach and watch yellow and black, long armed shovels digging in the sand at the shoreline looking for oil mats. What became known as the Avenida Incident among some locals, reveled 450 pounds of oil collected from a two mile stretch of the beach, from Avenida 10 and east.

We talked to a few locals on the beach that day, and none of them had a clue that BP was still collecting oil from the shorelines. Every one of them commented with, "What oil? The oil is gone. We don't know what you're talking about."

And these were people who worked or lived on the beach. And they were totally convinced that there was no oil, tar balls, or residue on the beach, let alone in the water.

Earth Day was celebrated on the third anniversary of the Deepwater Horizon Disaster, on Saturday, April 20th. On that day, the State of Florida announced that it was going to sue BP, and became the fourth gulf state to go after the oil giant. Mississippi filed their suit just the day before Florida. Halliburton was targeted as well.

The suit faulted BP for not charging the batteries on the blow out preventer. And Halliburton was charged with using faulty cement. And at this time, BP was still on trial in New Orleans, as a result of the Louisiana/Alabama law suit.

On April 22nd, as Celia and I drove onto the beach, we saw a dump truck and several bulldozers spreading sand onto the beach, as the dump truck unloaded. The dump truck then exited the island. I often wonder where they are getting the sand.

But I had to admit, the beach looked much cleaner after they were finished. And looking at the nasty black stained shores always saddens my heart. So even if they are hiding the effects that the oil had on our beach, it made it easier to see the good and unleash myself from all the negativity I had grown use to.

On May 14, 2013, Fox 10 News (WALA) was running a story regarding hundreds of fish floating onto the beaches from the Eastern Shore to Ft. Morgan, Alabama. As newscaster, Bob Grip was introducing the story, Lisa Ligon (newscaster) was nervously fumbling with something small in her hands. Which made the story seem rather concerning, as if her child, or a nephew, or someone she cared for had been swimming in that water earlier.

They interviewed Brian Hill of the Fort Morgan State Park, who had this to say, "The smell is pretty bad. People have been complaining that the beach is a mess, and we should clean it up. I don't have the staff or equipment to clean up this beach or anywhere to put them after we clean them up."

The interviewer went on to say, "According to the reports, the fish, redfish with some catfish have been found dead with no obvious signs of trauma." Not once was BP or the Deepwater Horizon Disaster mentioned as a possible cause. Or the fact that maybe the oil, Corexit, and/or tar balls may have something to do with it. Yet, it was the most obvious conclusion.

It was the second year in a row that large fish kills occurred in the same area. What did the fish test for last year? We're always told that test will tell us what happened, but we never hear the results of those test. Do you ever ask yourself, "Why?"

On May 18th, the 2013 Hands Across the Sand demonstration was held. Sassafrass, an environmental band consisting of two women, Jo Billups and Karen Harvill, played for a second year in a row, at the Pensacola event. The Gulf Shores, Alabama group represented as well.

The Alabama girls were concerned with tar sands that were to be delivered by rail to Mobile, Alabama that included 41 miles of pipeline that would run from Mobile to Moss Point, Mississippi. It would cross over 11 streams and 128 wetlands, jeopardizing Mobile's drinking water.

This was about the time I was introduced to the phrase, "Sacrifice Zone." Take for instance the asphalt that was collected from Ft. Pickens, where the road was washed away due to flooding. That asphalt was hauled to the east, five counties away, to Marianna, Florida, an African-American community.

And when you look at the larger picture, it is clear to see that the Southern States, as well as poor communities in general, are the sacrifice-zones for the rest of the countries addiction to energy dependence. Although Florida has been traditionally protected, the oil and gas industry was slowly worming their way into the state.

The EPA Thing

On May 24th, over the Memorial Day Weekend, the Pensacola News Journal published a Public Notice from the Environmental Protection Agency (EPA). Like most Floridian's I would have never been aware of the notice, due to entertaining friends from out of town, but a fellow activist did happen to see it and shared it with me right after the holiday weekend.

The EPA was seeking public comment on a draft of the Clean Air Act in which BHP Billiton Petroleum, Inc. (BHPB) was requesting a modification on their air permit. Why would this be a concern for the State of Florida, or the City of Pensacola?

Because the exploratory oil platform that BHPB was to build is directly South of Escambia County, 125 miles out in the Gulf of Mexico.

Historically, the Eastern Gulf of Mexico was protected from offshore drilling by a moratorium passed by Congress in 1982. The Gulf of Mexico Energy Securities Act of 2006, declared the Eastern Gulf off limits as well, until 2022. Furthermore, in December of 2010, the Obama administration reversed itself after the BP disaster, and promised not to pursue offshore drilling in the Eastern Gulf.

Imagine my surprise. The Gulf parcel itself had already been leased. No one seemed to be aware of the platform. And then again, if it was ever announced it was probably done in the same fashion that the EPA was using to post their announcement for public comment.

If you were to choose a day of the week in which almost no one would spot a public notice in the newspaper, I would say the Friday of Memorial Day weekend would be a excellent choice! No one's reading the paper. They're busting a nut to get out of town.

The only option available to the public was to challenge the Clean Air Act. I knew it was a long shot, due to all the secrecy and witnessing the behavior greed can have on people for the past couple of years. But I couldn't let the fight pass me by.

We had until June 10th to request a hearing with the EPA. They were accepting public comments until June 24th.

At first, I waited for the head of 350.org Pensacola to lead the way. She was given a copy of the announcement from the newspaper the same day I was provided with a copy. But I never heard anything. So then I gave a Facebook activist a copy of the announcement and asked her to post and share. Thinking she would lead the way. But I never seen or heard anything more about it.

I really didn't want to be the leader of this event. I was meditating a lot at the time. In meditation I was shown to let go of the past and to focus on the spiritual. But I couldn't in good conscious allow this act of harm on the environment to continue without doing anything.

So on June 5th, just five days before a hearing could be requested, I phoned the EPA and requested a hearing. I spoke with Art Hofmeister. He told me that he would have to have a considerable amount of requests, before they spent a bunch of money to travel down to Florida for a hearing.

So I posted an event page on Facebook called, "Defending Florida." At first, it was all about sending e-mails and calling the EPA requesting a hearing. The page/event got quite a lot of attention right away.

One girl, who had once accused me of using her husband's video in one of my videos, because my feet just so happen to look like his feet, had actually contacted the Sierra Club and 350.org to challenge the legitimacy of my post. She commented that neither one of those organizations knew anything about offshore drilling directly south of us.

That's how hard it was to believe that such a thing was happening. We were still reeling from the Deepwater Horizon disaster. Florida has a moratorium against offshore drilling; how could this be?

The Facebook chatter was all about Florida that day. People from all the Gulf States were in awe, "We can't allow this to happen. We'll have no where left to go to enjoy the beach."

Face it. The coastlines and beaches in Texas, Louisiana, Mississippi, and Alabama look like toxic waste lands in comparison to Florida. These people know that, and they missed what they use to have. They've seen the devastation that the oil and gas industry has had on their environment.

Pensacola beach has never looked the same since the Deepwater Horizon Disaster.

The next day, after contacting me, 350.org Pensacola began a Facebook event page as well. My thoughts were that it would be beneficial for an organization to represent; giving the event creditability.

But Elaine Sargent worked a full time job and did not have the time to lead the way. So I worked it.

On June 12th, Art Hofmeister granted us a hearing on the matter, for Thursday, June 27th, from 3 p.m. until 7 p.m. The EPA reported that 32 people requested a hearing.

I continued to work Facebook every morning posting something new to keep the event page in people's minds. I posted information regarding the hearing on Sierra Clubs Facebook page and other environmental pages. I worked YouTube too. I contacted environmental attorneys across the state, via email. We passed out flyers at area events here in Pensacola. The flyers contained contact information in case people couldn't make it to the hearing. I also contacted WEAR TV and requested they post a public notice on their daily bulletin board.

Then there were the signs that had to be made for the protest we planned right before the hearing. I poured my heart into this hearing, because I knew there would be no more chances to stop the oil and gas industry from kicking in the door and drilling off the shores of Florida. It was now, or never. Do or die.

The day of the hearing, there were fifteen of us who protested in front of the public library, where the hearing was to take place. One couple was from south Florida. Sassafrass was there (from Mississippi and Alabama); strumming their guitars and singing, "We don't need dangerous dirty energy. We stand together for the land and sea."

WEAR TV was there, and like every other time, I was the only one brave enough to be interviewed. I really didn't like speaking to reporters on camera, but everyone was pointing their fingers at me.

It was a peaceful protest, but a couple of community leaders entered the library from the back door and had nothing to do with the protest at all. I found it somewhat disheartening. The positive energy wasn't shared by all.

Art Hofmeister, the man who was to make the final decision, didn't even show up. The EPA representatives basically started the hearing by saying they weren't waiving any laws to amend BHPB's permit, as if the public notice was given for no reason.

That just didn't make any sense to me. And I'm sure they used the Facebook event page against us, because there were actually people discussing this very issue on the page. Yet the facts were, this company had to get their permit amended because they were omitting far more carbon then originally stated when they began the project. They had to get permission from the EPA for a reason! And the EPA posted the public notice for a reason!

One community leader began her speech by saying, "I came here today and wrote this statement, but you're not waiving the Clean Air act. And frankly my argument was based on that, because I knew that is how we would win at this case. It seems it's already decided."

She began to read here speech, but then went on to say a second time, "I don't know if my statement is going to make a big difference today, since the Clean Air Act, as you say, does not be weighed. And that is the power that is in your hands."

I cringed in my chair as she so easily declared defeat. I found myself wishing she had not spoken at all.

I practiced saying the words for my statement two days before the hearing. A little shaky, I rose to the podium and spoke from my heart. It went a little something like this -

"You know, when I was a freshman in high school, we had to take a Civics class as part of the curriculum. I loved that class and how the U.S. Constitution was explained to us. Checks and Balances, and all that.

And that is exactly what we are asking you to do today. To balance the playing field. You have the power to say no to this oil company. And set an example that we will not sacrifice any more of our precious resources for greed. That includes our air.

This past fall, my step-children and a grandchild came to visit us. Their mother took them to the beach to admire the sunset. When they returned, they all had sore throats.

When I go out on the beach, if the wind is blowing from the South or Southwest, I get a nagging cough. And most times, I even get a sore throat. Which is where the wind was blowing from that day my wife took the kids to the beach.

We haven't even begun to recover from the damage the Deepwater Horizon has caused to our environment, and yet there's an oil company requesting that we risk our health and possibly our livelihood for the soul purpose of oil. We're not dumb, we know there are alternative sources of energy.

Haven't we learned anything from the largest environmental incident to ever take place in the United States? We know de-regulation is not the answer. For sure!

You know, when I sit here and talk to you, I see an intelligent human being. Yet, we the people have to form a citizens collation to get Corexit, and other toxic oil dispersants removed from the EPA's approved list of dispersants, because the EPA has no procedure in place to do so. Do you realize how incredibly stupid that sounds to the average citizen?

You're suppose to be working for us. Not against us!

We use to be able to pull air quality data from a regional internet site, but that data was removed shortly after the Deepwater Horizon blew. And it is still unavailable to this day.

We know we have poor air quality here. We knew that before the Deepwater Horizon Disaster.

The Clean Air Act was put in place for a reason. Every American is aware of the Climate Crisis. It's affecting us all.

From a legal standpoint, I insist that you uphold the "Clean Air Act," and deny BHP Billiton OCS's permit that will waive the air quality standards that are in place.

But, from one human being to the next - I ask you not to allow

BHP Billiton OCS, or any other oil company that builds offshore platforms, to steal our breath away from us. Because we do not have any more to give.

Thank you for your time."

Mary Gutierrez, an Environmental scientist, and the Executive Director of Earth Ethic's Inc. spoke afterwards. She said she began as a chemist testing some of the parameters that were on the list that the EPA had provided us, at the beginning of the hearing. She said, "These parameters and pollutants are not foreign to me. I am quite well aware of the environmental and public health impacts associated with them. And I know this forum is to speak particularly for the increase of some of these parameters. And I would like to strongly urge you to deny this request to increase these parameters as listed here. Because of I know of the environmental impacts and the public health ramifications. And as stated before by some of the other speakers, this area has a long history of health issues, environmental issues, and we certainly do not need an increase in any of these things."

When the EPA called for a fifteen minute break, one of the reps approached me and questioned me about the web sites that use to report the air quality in the area. She referred me to someone else with the EPA, who could provide me with an internet address, but the only web address they gave me was to the front page of the EPA's web site, which is very hard to maneuver through. I never did find the page. And truthfully, I don't know if I would believe anything the EPA told me, especially after we were notified that we lost our battle, on July 11th.

The EPA said they received 88 comments total (via email, letter, or orally at the hearing). In part, the EPA's response read, "More than 60 (comments), explicitly opposed offshore drilling and/or drilling offshore Florida, or expressed sentiments that could be interpreted as general opposition to offshore drilling."

Furthermore, "None of the comments identified the CAA

(Clean Air Act) provisions, air quality standards, or regulations that the commenter believed EPA proposed to waive. Several commenter's indicated that these statements were in response to a citizen's Facebook post or flyer indicating that the EPA was "waiving" the CAA or air quality standards in this action. Nonetheless, no CAA provisions, air quality standards, or regulations were waived in this permit action. The EPA followed the applicable permit modification procedures of 40 CFR § 71.7(e)(3)."

I was at that hearing until 5 p.m., and I can tell you that not one "commenter" mentioned the Facebook page or the flyer I designed and passed out. And I have video of everyone who had spoken up to that point, except for my own comment. When we left at five, there was no one else there to speak. But the EPA did say they would be there until 7 p.m. regardless. And I know of at least one other individual who spoke after we had left.

As for Mary Gutierrez's statement, the EPA had this to say, "With respect to the comment that the EPA deny BHPB's request because of "the environmental impacts and the public health impacts," the commenter did not provide any substantive information or data related to the environmental or public health impacts of the proposed permit action, but rather generally referred to the health concerns raised by other speakers that were generally attributed to the Deepwater Horizon incident."

The EPA's response was eight pages long. The entire administrative record can be accessed at through the EPA's website at:
http://www.epa.gov/region4/air/permits/ocspermits/ocspermits.html.

As Elaine Sargent put it, "Live and learn." This was the first time any of us had ever challenged the EPA.

Still, if only 88 people responded with comments to the EPA, then there was clearly a lack of support to protect the very air we breathe. I was left feeling disappointed and defeated. What crushed my heart the most were those activists who didn't believe we could win from the word go. If they would put in half the effort they put into their daily complaining of the environment, into action, then we would be a powerful force to deal with.

Instead, protest became social events; a chance to get together and do lunch, or party for a while. Suddenly it was accepted behavior to be fashionably late to a protest. Like standing with a sign in your hand for half hour was any kind of a true sacrifice.

Sacrifice

The word sacrifice actually derives from the Latin word "Sacrum facere," which means "to make sacred." It's the act of giving up something dear, such as ones time, for something more worthy, like a cause that all of humanity can benefit from. As the Natives say, "Think seven generations ahead."

Sacrifice for your children, and their children's children. Think of their futures. Children shouldn't have to sacrifice for the life you want. Instead, you should be the one sacrificing, so your children can live the life they deserve.

True sacrifice is a victory, because it requires free will. It is an act of love; to love something more than your self.

The act of sacrificing is a universal law. By sacrificing you are getting rid of the old and making way for the new. The law of sacrifice explains why some people can not find success, or are in poor health. On an unconscious level, they are not willing to sacrifice to receive something new.

Sacrifice is not limited to heroes and saints; it is a necessary need in order to live a healthy life. To avoid disaster, to ourselves and our descendents, we must resist many of our desires, because sacrifice is the law of life.

Just two days before the EPA Hearing in Pensacola, Cherri Foytlin announced that she would be spending more time with her six children, and less time on the front lines fighting the gas and oil industry. Her words, "I have to let some things go."

For me, it just reinforced what I had felt back in May. It was time to change. It was time to let go of the old and reach for the new.

Mike Chenier, who played a big role in the creation of Idle No More Gulf Coast, fell out of the picture at this time too. Mike, who lived near New Orleans, was plagued with health issues after the Deepwater Horizon Disaster. Mike communicated with the tribes from Canada, and was the man who kept everyone connected. He was a friend to everyone. And his presence and inspiration were sorely missed.

Although Mike dropped off the map altogether, Cherri still blogged and posted on Facebook from home when she had the time. And as much as I just wanted to disappear, I still found myself representing to an extent as well.

Right after the EPA hearing on June 27th, Dot Schwartz told me that she and her husband had been swimming in the Gulf of Mexico during the Memorial Day weekend, and they both became very sick at the same time. Although she would not share her story with the EPA, she did allow me to video tape their story and post it on YouTube.

Dot and Dave had lived in Southern Florida for some time, before relocating back to Pensacola. Memorial Day was the first time they had swam in the Gulf since the 1990's. Their story goes like this:

"We got in the Gulf, we were fully immersed. Body surfing, head under the water and all that. And that night we both woke up with our throats, like razor blades in our throats, "said Dot.

"Almost like an anaphylactic, where your throat wants to close," interrupted David.

"Sinus, ear problems, pressure in the sinuses. The really funny thing was is we had been around no one who was sick. I have never had sinus problems, never had an ear ache, I rarely in my whole life ever got a sore throat. So I found it pretty coincidental that we got into the Gulf and then became sick," Dot continued.

"Actually to me," said David, "what was coincidental at time was we both were, we felt exactly same thing at pretty much the same time. So we figured, you know, what did we do that was in common? That was the one thing we hadn't done, in ages. And the thing is, the day seemed, the water looked beautiful. I mean it really looked nice. I didn't see any issues . . . there were no smells."

Anyone who knows David Schwartz would know that it takes facts to convince him of anything. This includes the use of Corexit in the Gulf of Mexico, in which their symptoms corresponded to exposure. For him to sit down and to be video taped is a statement in itself.

Dot, who was once a nurse, has a Masters degree in traditional Chinese medicine. They both farm, and they have chickens too. They pretty much live off the land.

"By the time we got home," David continued.

"We woke up in the night. In the middle of the night" added

Dot.

"It came on suddenly and simultaneously," said David.

"So we were sick for two weeks," Dot tallied.

Other information that became available in June was the National Oceanic and Atmospheric Administration (NOAA) report that forecasted, "this years Gulf of Mexico hypoxit *(hypoxic)* "dead" zone would be 7,286 and 8,561 square miles." Which would place it among the ten largest ever recorded.

Seismic testing for oil in the Gulf was a major issue in June as well. Seismic testing is deafening to marine life, especially for dolphins and whales, which depend on sonar to communicate. Seismic testing is a 100,000 times louder than a jet engine. Another explanation as to why dolphin strandings are high along the northern Gulf coast.

Despite thousands of signatures and petitions addressed to the Bureau of Ocean Energy Management (BOEM), three environmental groups agreed to a proposal that would allow testing to be done, except in three areas critical to whales and along the coast during calving season for bottle nosed dolphins, for 2.5 years.

On June 17th, a swimming advisory was issued for Navarre Park. Followed by another on June 28th; WEAR TV announced a water quality advisory regarding Shoreline Park in Gulf Breeze, Florida, due to high bacterial levels (same area).

Like I said though, it was time to use new eyes, and I found myself photographing and video taping drum circles, with fire dancers, and hoopers. I even involved the people who stood with me for Idle No More in a video contest that Nahko & Medicine For the People were pitching. It was all about lip-synching to their song,

Budding Trees.

We had a blast. It was fun. And it even gave me a chance to share our Gulf Water Blessing in the video. I liked the idea of getting more people involved with blessing the water. If more people did it, our oceans, rivers and lakes would be much happier, I'm sure.

But on July 12th, while shooting the Budding Trees video, you just couldn't miss the blackness of the shoreline, on Perdido Key State Park beach. So we decided to make the BP oil spill part of our video's theme as well.

And why not? We were emerging from the old into a new way of being. There is a lot of energy that goes into organizing a protest and constantly fighting a system of government that is corrupt from the bottom to the top.

Nahko's music is all about changing your frequency and using new eyes to see. His words truly have a healing effect. He and his crew are truly gifted. You can access all of their music on YouTube. Including, "Dark As Night," their debut CD, released just this year (2013).

As I looked around me, I could see the change that I felt. The people were waking and becoming aware. I was suddenly surrounded by young, expressive, imaginative people who were flowing with colorful hoops that glowed in the dark, while others flamed with chains that danced and circled around them in the air.

When I began sharing these colorful moments on Facebook, I was attacked by some. One guy called us a bunch of attention whores. He couldn't believe that we were promoting the beach, by sharing photos of a full moon drum circle.

I tried to explain to him that this was good for the beach, as well as for us. But he was down right rude and hateful.

I blew him off. But soon afterwards, I noticed activist who were Facebook friends, were no longer on my friends list. I found this somewhat disturbing, but all the same, I received many new requests once I began shooting video of the Pensacola Hoop Tribe, and Up In Flames Entertainment.

There's that theme again - "Let go of the old, and make way for the new."

Still, that didn't mean I no longer defended Mother Earth. I was still video taping, whenever I saw something on the beach.

After reading an article in the Pensacola News Journal (PNJ), on August 27th, regarding thousands of huge sea slugs that washed up on the beach, I did one such video.

University of West Florida (UWF) told PNJ that this is a natural occurrence. Quote, "Susan Teel, the Gulf Islands National Seashore chief of education, says the die-off actually is indicative of a healthy ecosystem."

Yet locals were left scratching their heads in wonderment. I even witnessed non BP believers supporting the fact that something wasn't adding up. You can call it what you want, but Gulf of Mexico is anything but healthy. Not when you look at the whole picture.

So I created a video with a timeline to show people just how often these die offs are occurring now as well as other news regarding the gulf. The date, place and incident scrolled up the screen, one after the other. Other than what I told you so far, other incidents included:

July 1, 2013, Biloxi, Mississippi; Massive Fish Kill.

July 4, 2013, Louisiana (no exact location given); Flesh Eating Bacteria.

August 1, 2013, Louisiana; Deepwater Horizon still leaking.

August 3, 2013, Tampa, Florida; Woman loses leg to flesh eating bacteria.

August 5, 2013, Researchers say that Sperm Whales in the Gulf of Mexico are the most polluted in the world.

August 20, 2013, Tampa Florida; Oil from the Deepwater Horizon found on the shelf in Tampa Bay.

August 25, 2013, Pensacola/Navarre Beaches; Massive Sea Slug die off.

And that is only what I know of, or what is reported. The flesh eating bacteria, also known as vibrio vulnificus, had hit the panhandle of Florida way before it was reported on the local news station, WEAR TV. We didn't hear anything about the person who died in Walton County, or the one who died in Okaloosa County.

And apparently vibrio vulnificus wasn't only a problem in the Gulf of Mexico, oyster beds in the cold waters of the New England, and the Pacific Northwest had to be shut down. Scientist believes that climate change may be contributing to the problem, due to the warming of the oceans.

In an article published by the Huffington Post (Joe Satran), on September 3rd, Dr. Jeff Duchin, Chief of Communicable Disease for Public Health Seattle and King County in Washington State had this to say, "This is probably the tip of the iceberg . . . for every case that is reported, an estimated 142 additional cases go unreported."

Vibrio Vulnificus is more common in the warm waters and is most prevalent in the summer months. It is most commonly associated with the consumption of raw oysters, but can be found in other shell fish as well.

If the bacterium is present in the water, avoid exposure to cuts on the skin. Eighty-four year old, Margaret Freiwald, who lost her leg, after swimming in the Gulf of Mexico near Tampa, was healthy as a horse, according to her daughter. Margaret cut her leg on the ladder, when climbing back in the boat.

I don't know if Margaret made it or not. It didn't sound good when a television station in Collier County reported the story. At that time, Margaret's kidneys were shutting down.

People with suppressed immune systems, including those with chronic health issues, such as liver problems, cancer, and sugar diabetes should avoid the water at all cost.

According to a microbiologist, Jim Oliver, Ph.D., if you catch the vibrio vulnificus bacteria, you have a fifty percent chance of dying, and if you do live you'll most likely lose your legs.

And the bacterium spreads fast. Henry Konietzky died within twenty-eight hours, after setting crab traps in the Halifax River, in Volusia County, Florida. Henry's wife said he had never been diagnosed with any health problems.

It was October 8th, when WEAR TV reported the first case of vibrio here in Escambia County. Less than twenty four hours later, another case was confirmed in Santa Rosa County.

October 10th, a case was confirmed in Mobile County, AL. At this time, there were 27 cases reported in the State of Florida. Nine people had died.

Then on October 11th, it was reported that there were two cases in Mobile County. Both men had been setting crab traps. One man died in late September, the other man had been hospitalized since October 6th.

At this time, on the eleventh of October, there were 32 confirmed cases and ten deaths in the State of Florida. The man in Santa Rosa County died, within two days of being reported.

On October 14th, WPMI, Local 15 News reported that a second man in Mobile County died from the flesh eating bacteria.

By October 30th, there had been 2 confirmed cases of exposure in Escambia County. 39 total reports, and 11 deaths within the State of Florida.

I myself became terrified to even collect water for the Gulf Blessing. I play with my cats and dogs quite a bit, and it isn't unusual for me to have cuts on my hands and arms. Not to mention the fire ants that has their way with my feet through out the year.

I never felt such fear of the water before. I began to wonder how much of this had to do with the Deepwater Horizon Disaster, so I pulled some figures from previous years, per the Florida Department of Health.

- 2008 – 15 cases – 05 deaths
- 2009 – 24 cases – 07 deaths
- 2010 – 32 cases – 10 deaths
- 2011 – 35 cases – 13 deaths
- 2012 – 27 cases – 09 deaths

➤ 2013 - 39 cases – 11 deaths (as of Oct 30th)

The Florida Department of Health has not updated their web site since October 30th. Considering how fast and furious the reports were coming in from local news sources through out the month of October, I question that these are the final figures for the year 2013.

After all, we are talking about a government that never provided the county with the results of water samples taken during the oil spill.

This brings me back to an Associated Press article published in March 2012, regarding tar balls and their relationship to the vibrio vulnificus bacteria.

As mentioned earlier, an Auburn University professor, Cova Arias found that the tar balls were teaming up with bacteria, including vibrio vulnificus. She found that "the balls had up 100 times more of that particular bacterium than the water they floated in and 10 times more than the sand they rested on."

When you consider that there are tar mats through out the Gulf of Mexico now, then it would make sense that to see an increase in the vibrio vulnificus bacteria.

Then add in the mix the fact that they are bringing sand in from somewhere off the island to refurbish the beach, due to erosion. Why not go offshore and throw the sand back onto the beach, as was done in the past?

Could it be because there is an eight mile tar mat right off **Pensacola Beach**, as rumored back in April?

I think common sense can dictate that anywhere there was oil on the oceans surface, there is most likely a tar mat sitting somewhere near by below, on the ocean floor.

On November 7th, WKRG News 5 (Mobile), interviewed Professor Arias, with regards to the flesh eating bacteria. It was your typical play it down kind of story. They downplayed the statistics considerably, broadcasting, "It effects about five people a year in Alabama, and about thirty in Florida, with a 40% death rate."

While there introducing the story, they show little kids digging in the sand along the shoreline, then flip the lens to tar balls laying in the wet sand.

Still, Dr. Arias advised not to touch tar balls with your bare hands, adding, "I would stay away from the waters."

The reporter went on to say, "And as Tropical Storm Karen washed in a new batch of tar balls last month, beach goers were oblivious to the dangers."

From locals to visiting Yankees, no one paid the tar balls any mind. "I was just looking for shells in the sand and came across it," said one lady. She was holding the tar ball in her hand, while her two year old son was running in circles around her, speaking baby talk.

Two other women from Prattville, Alabama had this to say, "Gotten em all over our fingers, and stepped on em, and gotten em all over our feet."

Then the reporter showed a huge tar ball, with a sharp pointy shell stuck to it. It just blew my mind! Oh my God, could you imagine someone stepping on that?

Dr. Arias said that there was no evidence that you can get vibrio from touching a tar ball, "but the possibility is there."

"The only thing we know is that they do have all the vibrios, particularly in the summer months. And they have more vibrios than sand or water"

The very next evening, the same broadcaster, WKRG News 5, ran a second story. This time they provided statistics from the Alabama Department of Health. The states chart only included reported cases of vibrio; no deaths.

- 2009   10 Cases
- 2010   03 Cases
- 2011   03 Cases
- 2012   04 Cases

"There have been almost two dozen cases of vibrio vulnificus, in Alabama, over the last five years (Note: only four years are listed). In Florida, one hundred and sixty cases during a recent six year period (2008-2013); a third of them deadly. An Escambia County man was killed by vibrio this summer," said the reporter.

What? An Escambia County man died this summer after being infected with vibrio? The Florida Department of Health statistics did not reflect an Escambia County man dying from vibrio this past summer.

Where are Alabama's figures for 2008 and 2013? How many fatalities? And what do you think the chances are that as vibrio statistics rise in the State of Florida, they decline in the State of Alabama? After all, we are speaking about a state that has had massive fish kills, in the spring, for the past two years.

Alabama's coastline is considerably smaller in comparison to Florida. But really, does such a decline, and after the BP oil spill of all things, makes sense to you?

Dr. Arias said, "What we also found was that in water the numbers were around ten times higher, than the numbers that had been reported before (the BP Oil Spill), from that area."

Then the camera cuts to the next scene, then the reporter cuts back in and tells the viewers, "So the water alone had ten times as much vibrio as before the oil spill. And remember the tar balls themselves had one hundred times the vibrio than the water."

I don't know if it was just plain bad reporting or just a bad job of convincing people that it was ok to swim in the gulf? Still, that is not what Dr. Arias said. And of course BP had this to say in regards to Dr. Arias' findings, "Dr. Arias study does not support a conclusion that tar balls may represent a new or important route of human exposure for the vibrio infection, or that the detection of vibrio in tar balls would impact the overall public health risk, since there are far more common sources of vibrio, such as seawater and oysters."

Dr. Arias said she would like to do more research, but did not have the funding to continue the study on tar balls.

On December 3rd, The Times- Picayune New Orleans reported that the Bureau of Ocean Energy Management (BOEM) will put up more than 465,000 acres in the Eastern Gulf of Mexico up for lease.

"The Obama administration has approved lease sales as far east as the Florida panhandle under its five year lease program rolled out in 2012."

This does not include the deepwater drilling already taking place just 50 miles off the Florida coast, thanks to Cuba.

Despite spending approximately $700 million dollars, in oil exploration over the past ten years, and coming up with nothing, Cuba is still determined to drill. Desperate for economic growth, the Cuban government is relying on seismic testing, which indicates that there is a large deposit north of the island. But the oil can be as deep as 10,000 feet or more, and their quest pushes further northward close to Florida shores.

If a major spill were to occur, the Gulf Stream current would most certainly drag the oil slick north, across coral reefs and into the Florida Keys.

CHAPTER SIX – Conclusion

The year 2014 began as a cold hard warning. Temps in Pensacola were dropping to eighteen degrees, with harsh northern wind chills. Polar Vortex became a new vocabulary word for many in the Eastern United States, including Florida. While we were freezing in the south, the state of Alaska had temps in the fifties and sixties.

In late January the panhandle of Florida was basically closed for three to four days, due to ice, of all things. All bridges were closed at one time or another during the storm, because the southern states do not have snow plows, or salt to melt the ice.

Interstate 10 was closed from the Alabama/Florida state line east to mile marker 233. But not until after five big rigs and twelve other vehicles collided over the bay. At least one vehicle plummeted into the dark frigid water below; killing three people.

A CSX train derailed in McDavid (northern Escambia County), with 23 cars crashing into Fletcher Creek. Two of the cars were carrying phosphoric acid. Although twelve homes were evacuated during the storm, no leaks from the wrecked cars were reported.

And that's just what happened during the storm, in my neck of the woods. That's not including interstate closures in Louisiana, Mississippi, Alabama and Georgia, or other accidents and fatalities that occurred in the Deep South.

During the Russian Winter Olympics, in February, the temps rose to sixty degrees on the slopes, while the United States was pounded with more extreme winter weather, descending as far south as Atlanta, Georgia.

Global Warming is now referred to as Climate Change; because some people can't wrap their minds around the fact that global warming refers to excessive weather patterns. They can't see the whole picture. They only see what is going on in their own immediate circle. The thought that if it's not sixty degrees in their backyard in the middle of winter leads them to believe global warming does not exist.

I don't know if Climate Change is a better label though. After all, the weather changes all the time. I can't remember ever seeing back to back winters being the same as the last.

But I do know that the weather is getting more and more extreme. In the twelve years that I have lived in Florida, I had never seen ice and sleet, other than once it snowed for less than a minute, in 2010. We had seen it all in January 2014 and not on the same day either. On two different occasions the temps didn't even rise above freezing during the day.

I look at the dead fruit hanging from the kumquat tree next door. It no longer has any leaves; just brown a barren. I don't know if it'll recover from the winter or not. I can't help but wonder what winters will be like ten and twenty years from now, if we continue to use fossil fuels like we are?

Just as fast as the thought occurs in my mind, I find myself chasing it away because no longer am I living, but instead, I am dying. There is no future without hope. It really does matter what eyes you use to view any situation.

Some people will tell you that humanity as whole will never change or evolve. And though it is easy to get sucked up into that thought, when we still wage war with one another, I search my mind for contradictions.

Take for example, the Gladiators of Rome, who would fight to the death to entertain the masses. Now, we have football. Although some would consider the modern day sport as barbaric, the violence in football is pale in comparison to the fatality rate of first century B.C. games of Rome. And more so today then ever there is a growing concern over head injuries that are associated with playing the game of football. Indicating more changes are on the way.

Speaking of head injuries, did you know that the human brain has shrunk over the past thirty thousand years? According to Phys.org, the loss is equal to the size of a tennis ball. That's evolution.

Here's another glimpse of evolution. Did you know that 95% of all the species that has ever lived on this planet are gone? That's right – extinct! We didn't kill them all, they just disappeared. That is the way nature operates. Now ask yourself why?

Is it possible they may have evolved into something greater? Kind of like the theory of man evolving from an ape.

Two million new species have been identified since 1758. It wasn't until 1869 when the panda bear was discovered. In a report by International Institute for Species Exploration at Arizona State University, 19,233 new species were discovered in 2009. Out of those 41 were mammals.

By no means am I supporting the death of thousands of sea life due to the neglect of mankind. Humanity has a responsibility to live in harmony with all. And when we see a wrong done against another human being, or an animal, or the living Earth, we have a duty to stand and raise our voices to set that wrong right.

For me, doing right by what I've seen in the past four years is protesting, photography, sharing a very personal story, and keeping an accurate record of this important time in history, when the media allows greed to dictate the truth.

Four is the number that represents foundations; it is a number to build upon. This year Easter falls on the 4 year anniversary of the Deepwater Horizon Disaster (April 20). Easter symbolizes death and resurrection. Indeed, a new day has arrived.

Showtime came out with a new weekly series in April 2014, called "Years of Living Dangerously." It was originally suppose to air on April 13th, but instead it was released on YouTube on April 6th, because the creators wanted to spread the message worldwide; not everyone can afford Showtime, and it is not available in every country. Maybe this is truly a sign of the end of greed.

Faith

Dream Journal Entry - Tuesday, February 15, 2005

I'm in a wooden house. There are people coming and going. There's a conveyor belt in the middle of the room. It brings water up into the house.

Next, I'm in the front yard of a stone house, and I want to get to the backyard. Some guy sees me and tells me if I like, I can cut through the house to get to the back yard. I walk into the house and into a large stone room. It's beautiful. There are two pillars and three windows. The windows are large (from the ceiling to the floor) and facing the backyard. I notice water from the ocean is splashing along the bottom of the windows. I wonder how it is the water does not leak into the house.

I walk to the windows and look out in awe. There's a giant conveyor belt that is bringing the water up to the house. There's children playing and climbing along the rafters. And right before I wake up, the name King Solomon is spoken.

Wood and stone; old and new; evolution - Solomon was the son of David. When David ruled, it was a time of war. But when Solomon reigned it was a time of peace.

The Catholic reading for the date of February 15, 2005; the morning I had the dream.

Isaiah 55:10-11, "Thus says the Lord: Just as from the heavens the rain and snow come down and do not return there till they have watered the earth, making it fertile and fruitful, giving seed to the one who sows, and bread to the one who eats, so shall my word be that goes forth from my mouth; it shall not return to me void, but shall do my will, achieving the end for which I sent it."

A friend had asked me why I felt compelled to write this book. And that is my answer, "I must do what I was sent here to do."

That's kind of what faith is all about. It's about believing in yourself, and in your dreams.

You are special. You wouldn't be here today, if you weren't. I need you. The world needs you! And God is speaking to you. Whether is be in dreams, or the people, places and animals you encounter throughout the day. Life truly is magical, when you learn the language.

There is a poem I found on the Internet long ago. I have no clue who wrote it. But it is too great of a lesson not to share. It is an example of how God speaks to us through His Creation:

The man whispered, "God, speak to me." And a meadowlark sang. But he man did not hear.

So the man yelled, "God speak to me!" And the thunder rolled across the sky. But the man did not listen.

Then the man looked around and said, "God, let me see you." And a star shined brightly. But the man did not notice.

And the man shouted, "God, show me a miracle!" And life was born. But the man did not know.

So the man cried out in despair, "Touch me God, and let me know you are here." Whereupon, God reached down and touched the man. But the man brushed the butterfly away and walked on.

So you see, God does speak to you through His Creation. Therefore, we have an obligation to respect that creation and to live in harmony with all living creatures. We have a duty to protect the water, the sea life, the air, the birds, the trees, the plants, and the four legged ones, as if they are our relatives.

Question what you see. What you dream. Unplug the computer and the television and any other distractions you have humming around you, and quiet your mind. Sit outside somewhere. Walk barefoot, with your feet touching the Earth, not asphalt or concrete. Talk to God, it's the best medicine.

If you would like to know more about how to communicate to the Creator through nature, I recommend a book by Ted Andrews called Animal Speak.

If I had to name a book to help you interpret your dreams, I would recommend Betty Bethards, The Dream Book, because it does have a dream dictionary included. But there are free online dream dictionaries available as well.

And now I say, "Aloha! Water the Earth and make it fertile and fruitful. Achieve what you were sent here to do."

In Honor of the Eleven Men Who Died With the Deepwater Horizon

April 20, 2010

✝

Jason Anderson (35)

Aaron Dale "Bubba" Burkeen (37)

Donald Clark (49)

Stephen Ray Curtis (40)

Gordon Jones (28)

Roy Wyatt Kemp (27)

Karl Kleppinger Jr (38)

Keith Blair Manuel (56)

Dewey A Revette (48)

Shane M Roshto (22)

Adam Weise (24)

THE NORTHERN GULF OF MEXICO

County Map of Northwest Florida

Alabama

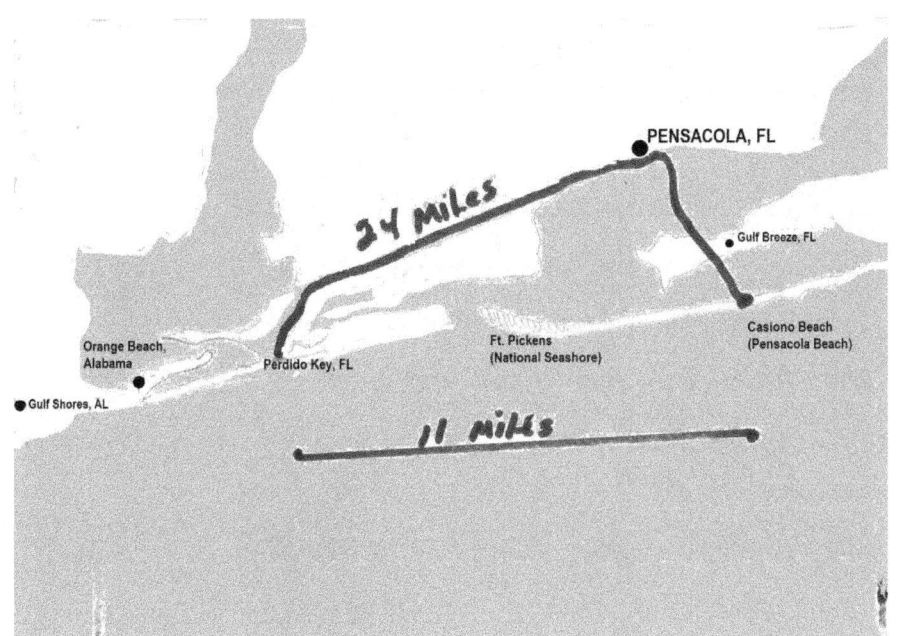

ON-LINE REFERENCE TO GULF OIL REPORTING

Florida

Gregg Hall - www.youtube.com/user/truereporting

Kim Schulz - www.youtube.com/user/WoMenHead101

Trisha Peters Williams - www.youtube.com/user/44gulfwaters

Trisha James - www.youtube.com/user/tjatnb

Alabama

John Wathen - www.youtube.com/user/hccreekkeeper

Mississippi

Denise Rednour - www.youtube.com/user/deniselngbch

Charles Taylor - www.youtube.com/user/MrFreezebear73

Laurel Lockamy - www.youtube.com/user/Lockamy1

Louisiana

Louisiana Environmental Action Network - leanweb.org

Save Our Gulf - saveourgulf.org

Bridge the Gulf - bridgethegulfproject.org

Gulf Restoration Network - healthygulf.org

TONY KENNON w/THE WASHINGTON POST

http://www.washingtonpost.com/wp-dyn/content/discussion/2010/06/15/DI2010061504608.html

www.ingramcontent.com/pod-product-compliance
Lightning Source LLC
Chambersburg PA
CBHW032128090426
42743CB00007B/515